Coaching Evelyn

Fast, Faster, Fastest Woman in the World

Coaching Evelyn

Fast, Faster, Fastest Woman in the World

by Pat Connolly

HarperCollins*Publishers*

Typography by Joyce Hopkins
1 2 3 4 5 6 7 8 9 10
First Edition

Library of Congress Cataloging-in-Publication Data
Connolly, Pat.
  Coaching Evelyn ; fast, faster, fastest woman in the world / by Pat Connolly.
    p.   cm.
  Summary: Ashford's coach describes the techniques and training regimen used to
develop the ability of a great American sprint champion.
  ISBN 0–06–021282–9. — ISBN 0–06–021283–7 (lib. bdg.)
  1. Ashford, Evelyn—Juvenile literature.   2. Runners (Sports)—
United States—Biography—Juvenile literature.   3. Connolly, Pat—
Juvenile literature.   4. Track-athletics—United States—Coaching—
Biography—Juvenile literature.   [1. Ashford, Evelyn.   2. Runners
(Sports)   3. Track and field.]   I. Title.
GV1061.15.A84C66 1991
796.42′2′092—dc20   90–4835
[B]   CIP
[92]   AC

Dedication

For my children, Brad, Adam, and Shannon, and for Raina Washington and all young people who must find their way by believing in themselves

Acknowledgments

My Olympic-sized thanks go to Harold, Mary Anne, Mr. Parker, and Sallie, without whom there would be no story, and to Zan and Marc, who coached me into writing it with encouragement and tough editing. Also thanks to Jon Hendershott and Harmon Brown for their help with the facts.

Contents

Coaching Evelyn

Fast, Faster, Fastest Woman in the World

CHAPTER ONE

Speed at First Sight

Only 5 feet 4½ inches tall and weighing less than 115 pounds, Evelyn Ashford seemed too small to be much of a runner—until she started to sprint. Then, as her speed increased, she appeared to grow tall. Her eyes were focused on a horizon only she could see. Her arms swung below her hips providing balance to her extra-long legs as they gathered up the ground with loose, effortless strides. Over the next nine years Evelyn's stature in the world of sports would grow tall as well. But it wasn't easy, and she would lose her best friend along the way.

I first saw Evelyn run in 1976, at UCLA's Drake Stadium. Drake, carved in a steep hillside just off Sunset Boulevard in Los Angeles, was surrounded on three sides by bushy pines and giant eucalyptus trees that freshened the normally smoggy air. The

metallic gold bleachers reflected the southern California sunshine illuminating the track. From these
stands I could see the brick, Ivy-League-style campus
that had been home to hundreds of famous male
athletes.

You can get to Drake by walking through the
turnstile in a chain-link fence that separates the
track from a large field that is used by student
leagues for games of soccer, softball, and touch
football, and for marching band practice. Danny,
the good-natured groundskeeper, was always
around back then. He kept the grass infield and
its surrounding rubberlike track in such tip-top
shape that even foreign athletes were drawn there
to test themselves under Drake's ideal conditions.
The University of California at Los Angeles was,
and still is, a public institution, and its track belongs
to all the people, not just to track-and-field athletes.
In the thousands of times I have been to Drake, it
has never been deserted. Other stadiums empty out
after each event. But at Drake, even in the heavy
fog of a winter midnight footsteps can be heard.

Only six miles west of Hollywood, Drake often
seemed to be just another set in the famous movie
town. Actresses and actors, directors and produc-
ers, famous politicians and professional sports stars
jogged along with the regular UCLA student-athletes (Bruins) in the real-life drama of Drake Stadium. The "extras" included soft-muscled starlets in
pastel headbands and leg warmers; pudgy football

players running with stopwatches in hand; rich housewives with time to kill; artists, writers, and professors dutifully jogging their daily laps.

On this cool January afternoon in 1976, the low winter sun was disappearing behind the trees, casting their shadows over the bleachers and across the track. Only a few others were on the coral-colored track when I met my Bruin team for the first time. I'd been asked to coach the women's track-and-field team in the middle of the school year after the coach who had been in charge of the women, quit cold. He'd said, "Coaching women is a pain. They have too many excuses for missing practice, like bellyaching about their menstrual cramps."

The rejected Bruin team of about eighteen women was seated in the bleachers. "Hi. I'm Pat Connolly, your new coach." I stood facing them with what I hoped was a posture of confidence. "Many people don't take women athletes seriously, but I do, and I expect you to do so as well. Congress has passed legislation called Title IX, without which neither you nor I would be here. Before Title IX only men could get athletic scholarships to compete for their colleges. Now, all publicly funded schools must give women the same chance to compete that they offer to men. Title IX is the best thing that has happened to women athletes in the U.S. But we must prove that we deserve this chance. I'll be asking you to do things that may seem impossible. But, in time you'll be able to do them. Women athletes have not yet been challenged. I expect you to work harder than the men's team. You can take me seriously.

"As for my experience, I used to coach at Beverly Hills High School. Before that I competed on three Olympic teams—in the eight hundred meters and the pentathlon. But enough of me. It's getting chilly. I want to see you run, put the shot, and do the standing long jump and high jump. I'll be timing each of you in every distance from the hundred meters to the mile."

"Mile?" shouted a tall, slender runner from the back row.

"Oh, no!" came the groans. Athletes hate to be timed in distances other than their favorite races.

"No way you're gonna make me run that far. I'm a sprinter! Sprinters don't run the mile," said the same girl, whose teammates were nodding in agreement.

"Your times in these trials are not important to your status on the team. I just want to evaluate your strength, endurance, speed, and form. For today you'll be timed only in the hundred meters. So relax."

The athletes jogged off to begin their warm-up, and the band began practicing on the field that separated the track from the campus. As I walked down to the center of the track keeping time to the music, I was filled with the same anticipation I had felt as a six-year-old on Christmas Eve.

A slim, quiet girl I hadn't noticed during the meeting in the bleachers was last to try out. She waited patiently beside me for her turn to run. When I asked her name, she said, "Evelyn Ashford," succinctly pronouncing each syllable.

"How old are you?" I asked.

"Eighteen."

"Did you run in high school?"

"They didn't have a girls' team." Evelyn's tiny wrists, small waist, and slender ankles reminded me of a delicate porcelain figurine. Only her large Afro hairstyle did not fit her streamlined appearance.

"So. Where have you run before?"

She seemed not only shy but reluctant to talk to me. Finally she said, "In high school I raced and beat the boys at lunchtime. The boys' track coach asked me to be on his team."

"Well, let's see you run. Do you have racing spikes with you?"

"No, only my flats." She walked slowly to the top of the straightaway.

By standing in the middle of the infield, I could see the athletes from the front, side, and back as they ran down the 100-meter straight. Running fast appears easy, but it's hard, especially at top speed, when sprinters must overcome the fear of falling that increases with their speed. Holding my stop-watch down at my side, I watched the shy, reluctant talker start to run.

Surprise, then wonder, came over me as Evelyn accelerated to full speed. I knew, yes positively knew, that she could be great, perhaps even the best sprinter of all time. Though her stride was too long and her arms were carried low, her body was in balance and fast, so fast she almost blurred with the chain-link fence behind her. As she slowed to a stop, I looked at my watch. Unbelievable! Eleven point seven seconds! How could she be that fast without spikes, on the first day of practice? Maybe I flubbed her time?

"Wow, she looks great," yelled Karin Smith as she drilled her javelin straight into the ground beside her for emphasis. Karin was a three-time junior USA javelin champion who'd just enrolled at UCLA.

"She certainly does! But I missed her time. This can't be right," I said as I started to walk toward the little runner with the big stride. Glancing at my clipboard to remember her name I said, "Evelyn, please come over here."

A runner on the men's team called out to her, "Way to go," but she just looked down at her feet and kept walking.

"You have a beautiful running style with forward

Students stop their activities to watch a young Ashford win a collegiate meet at Drake.

lean that reminds me of Olympic champion Wyomia Tyus. But my watch can't be right. Could you please run it for me again so I can be sure of your time?"

"OK," she said without hesitation.

For verification I gave one of my stopwatches to Karin, who whistled in amazement when she read Evelyn's second trial time. We both had the same clocking—11.7. Evelyn's speed was for real, as were the butterflies that would tickle my stomach practically every time I watched her run from then on.

That night I couldn't wait to tell my husband, Harold, about Evelyn. "The best sprinter I have ever seen tried out for my team today."

As usual when I was excited about something, he was skeptical. "You mean better than Tyus or Rudolph?" We both knew these Olympic champions who'd raced for Tennessee State University.

"Better than Jesse Owens! If she trusts me and has patience, someday she can win Olympic gold. She can break the world record—everything."

Harold was correcting essays by his high school English students. He looked up over the top of his reading glasses. "Who are you kidding? The Olympic trials are less than six months away. She can't beat the new sprinters from Tennessee State."

A 1956 Olympic champion in the hammer throw

Karin Smith, handkerchief, watch, and javelin, warms up for a meet at Drake Stadium.   Bill Leung and a former coach of the Santa Monica High School boys' track team, Harold knew track. But was he being fair? Were my hopes too high? Would I have trouble convincing people of what I knew? Harold's doubts made me realize that I had better not talk publicly about Evelyn's exceptional talent. If I expected too much of her, it would only hurt her. Yet I fell asleep that night thinking about Evelyn's long, smooth stride that pulled in the track like no other. Watching her develop would be like watching my favorite Olympic sport, figure skating. Having studied ballet, I'd always been thrilled to see the effortless flow and grace that ice and skates add to what would otherwise be a mere dance. Evelyn was that fluid.

CHAPTER TWO

Warming Up

Vivacious Karin Smith was the first athlete to visit me in my office that week. The office lights may still be flickering from her radiant smile. I had seen this remarkable javelin thrower from La Jolla, California, compete in a local track meet. With her long brown hair jabbing out in all directions and a bright-red handkerchief tied around her neck, she had thrown the javelin like it was a live stick of dynamite. Now, in my office, she wore short hair and sat almost still. After telling me she hoped to make the Olympic team that year, she questioned me. "What do you know about coaching the javelin?"

"Karin, I've competed in or coached every event in women's track and field except the javelin. I don't even know how to grip the javelin, much less teach you how to throw it."

Karin's smile faded. Confusion and disappointment crept over her face.

"What I do know is how to get you in the best shape of your life so that you'll be stronger and more explosive than you've ever been. I can also help you prepare your mind for competition. And I'll find and consult with a javelin expert to assist you with your throwing technique."

Karin had not expected such candor; many coaches try to bluff their athletes by pretending to know everything. She'd met some of these pretender coaches, who'd tried to recruit her to their teams.

"You'll have a better chance of making the Olympic team than most of your competitors. I'm ready to do whatever it takes, within the rules, to see that you have the opportunity to achieve your goals. The rest is up to you."

"No problem. I like work." Karin's engaging smile took possession of her face once again. "Has Evelyn Ashford come in for her visit yet?"

"No, but she's scheduled to be here soon. Do you know her?"

"A little. She was on a USA Junior National team with me last summer. She ran the relay but wasn't noticed because Tennessee State stars Brenda Morehead and Chandra Cheeseborough were dazzling everyone with their times."

"Well, Karin, I know Coach Temple, and he probably thinks Brenda and Chandra are his next great sprinters." (At Tennessee State, Coach Temple had produced Olympic champions Wilma Rudolph, Wyomia Tyus, and Edith McGuire.) "Chandra has already broken the world record for Juniors in the one hundred and two hundred meters. Besides, I think Coach Temple likes his sprinters taller than Evelyn. Rudolph was nearly six feet." To myself I said, "It's going to be fun beating the great Mr. Temple with an athlete he neglected!"

Quickly learning how to read my face, Karin asked, "You think Coach Temple made a mistake ignoring Evelyn last summer? Can she make the team this year?" We both knew that she meant the Olympic team, and her question was hard for me to answer. If I said yes, that would put tremendous pressure on Evelyn. If I said no, I wouldn't be showing confidence. But this time I went out on a limb and said, "Evelyn and *you* have the ability to make the team, but you must want it more than your competitors do. You must also have some luck."

Pleased with my answer, Karin glanced at the big watch on her wide red wristband and said, "I've gotta go to class now." I stayed to meet with other members of my team. Diane Kummer soon walked in, flashing the second biggest smile I'd ever seen. Her straight brown hair was as shiny as her smile. The thought crossed my mind that maybe I could get a shampoo or toothpaste company to help sponsor my athletes. Budgets for most women's teams were inadequate, and I'd been seeking ways to raise extra funds for travel, uniforms, and equipment.

Diane was a long jumper who'd come to UCLA from Chicago. She had jumped more than twenty feet when she was just sixteen years old. She also was an aspiring Olympian, but her event was loaded with tough competitors, including Willye White, her fellow Chicagoan. An Olympic silver medalist, Willye would be trying for her sixth Olympic team that year. With many other talented long jumpers vying for three spots on the team, Diane's chances were not good. Long jumping combined speed with power and lift. It was my favorite event, and having been a national long-jump champion myself, I knew what Diane needed.

"You'll have to eat, drink, and sleep long jumping—after your schoolwork that is," I told her. Then, as with all my athletes, we spoke of academic goals, class schedules, and other student-athlete problems.

But her mind quickly went back to track. "Don't you think that with Ashford, we can be awesome in the sprint relays?"

"Yes, and you'll run the third leg, passing the baton to Evelyn."

Long jump and sprinting were my favorite events, though you can't tell from the look on my face.   AP/Wide World Photos

Evelyn herself was the last to come in for an office visit that day. What had been her large Afro hairstyle at Drake Stadium was now a neatly styled perm, the kind of "do" her mother might have given her. I sat at my desk reminding myself not to overwhelm her with my enthusiasm. I spoke first. "Hi."

She smiled and replied with a warm "Hi." I noticed for the first time that she had slightly chipped teeth with a space between the front two, just like my own chipped gappers. So much for the toothpaste sponsor I'd hoped for.

"How did you happen to choose UCLA?" I began.

"It was the only school that offered me a scholarship."

"You've got to be kidding! With your ability to score team points in five events, I can't believe you weren't offered several scholarships."

"I wanted to go to Tennessee State, but Coach Temple never talked to me."

"Mr. Temple might realize his mistake someday."

"What do you mean?" Evelyn kept her large brown eyes locked on mine.

"I mean that if you want to be the best, you will be. I mean that Chandra and Brenda will see a lot of your backside before they finish competing!"

Evelyn laughed and sat back in her chair but didn't say much. It was years before I was able to find out details of her background. Her father, Sam

Ashford, was a Senior Master Sergeant in the United States Air Force. Evelyn, born in Shreveport, Louisiana, had lived with Sam and her mother, Vietta, in Okinawa, Morocco, Texas, Mississippi, Ohio, Missouri, and Alabama. Evelyn's younger brother, Richard, and her three younger sisters, Joy, Wanda, and Eunice, had each been born in different cities. I eventually learned that it was Mrs. Ashford who kept the family together while her husband was on secret assignments in Vietnam, and that while in the Philippines, Evelyn's dad had earned his black belt in karate.

Fortunately Sgt. Ashford had been stationed near Sacramento, California, for Evelyn's high school days. At Roseville High the boys' track coach, Gary Genzlinger, had put Evelyn on his team after seeing her beat all challengers in lunchtime races that she ran for extra helpings of dessert. She surprised other high schools by beating their boys on her leg of the relay. Some opposing coaches had protested when they realized that Roseville's second runner in the relay was a girl.

One rival coach, Will Stevens, who first saw Evelyn run with the boys at their regional championships, didn't complain. He coached a successful girls' track team, and he invited Evelyn to be one of "Will's Spikettes." A big teddy bear of a coach, Will was respected and loved by his athletes. He took Evelyn to the Junior National Championships in 1975, where she placed fourth, making her a member of the Junior National relay team. Coach Stevens also helped her get the scholarship to UCLA.

"Have you considered trying out for the Olympics this year?" I wanted to know what her goals were.

"No way. Me? No way," she scoffed.

"Why not?"

"I'm not that good."

"Yes, you are. Don't worry about Brenda and Chandra. There are three spots on the team. Four spots counting the relay. If you could, would you like to go to Montreal as a member of the United States Olympic Team?"

"Sure. I always wanted to be like Wilma Rudolph." Wilma was the legendary sprinter who had won three gold medals at the Rome Olympics in 1960, and every American woman sprinter since then has run in Wilma's shadow.

I hesitated momentarily before saying, "I trained with Skeeter — Wilma — when we were both on the Olympic team, and I believe you can run faster than she did in Rome. But it has to be *your* dream, not just mine. Competition in the sprints is tougher now, especially from the East Germans. It may take you years to realize your dream. You must keep a positive attitude, and, of course, not miss practice."

Our eyes locked, and from that moment on it was clear that we would communicate more with our expressions than with spoken words. There was now a flicker of hope in Evelyn's eyes as they responded to the conviction coming from my baby blues. I ended the conference with: "At practice this afternoon we'll be learning a new warm-up. See you then."

"OK. 'Bye." Evelyn picked up her books and left my office.

That afternoon I warned my team, "I am not going to kill anyone, but our practices will be so tough sometimes you might wish you were dead. You all had to be good students to be admitted to UCLA, so I expect you to ask questions when you don't understand me. We won't be doing the same old workouts that other teams are doing. We will not copy men's programs. What the men do isn't always right for us. I have a lot of new ideas about training. Some of them come from European and Soviet coaches and athletes. Other approaches I've taken from my study of ballet. To be the best, we must take some chances and we must not make the same blunders twice. You'll be ahead of the game if you can learn from the mistakes I've already made as an athlete."

Eventually the team would like my long lectures, because listening to them gave them a break from their workouts. They'd laugh in all the right places and add their own jokes and encourage me to repeat stories from my Olympic days. But that afternoon I was all business.

"UCLA is sponsoring this team, and our athletic director is looking for big team success at the collegiate championships. Nevertheless, I'll be coaching you as individuals, not with team scoring in mind. This is an Olympic year. Those who qualify for the Olympic trials will be at their peaks in June instead of in May for the college championships. Now let's get started with your new warm-up."

My status as an Olympian along with my straight-forwardness made it easy for me to gain the team's respect, which is an important ingredient of coaching. (Women coaches don't get the automatic homage that men coaches do, even from other women.) At thirty-three years of age I was still young and fit enough to take my team through the entire warm-up without getting as tired out as they did. The number and variety of exercises and drills seemed endless to them. We did build-ups, knee lifts, speedy feet, skips, bounds, hops, kick butts, sit-ups, push-ups, froggies, donkey kicks, step-ups, shake-ups, and more. All of these became a daily ritual for each of them.

"This warm-up is longer than my whole work-out," cried sprinter Gayle Butler.

When I first demonstrated the dangling-arm quick-stepped shake-up, they all laughed. "Nobody runs like that," said Karin. Even Evelyn piped up: "You've got to be kidding!" None of them failed to notice my boobs bouncing from side to side. So when I asked them to try it, Diane Kummer said, "The men are gonna laugh at us."

"Let 'em laugh. When we're winners they'll quit laughin' and start copyin'."

I have to admit I laughed too as I watched their first attempts to do shake-ups, a quick-tempo drill that we ran barefoot on the grass infield. Some looked like penguins. Others goose-stepped like German soldiers. Only Evelyn could do it without looking like her pants had dropped to her ankles. She soon was covering the 100-meter distance of each shake-up quite quickly.

When I yelled, "You've got to relax more," Gayle flopped on the ground saying, "This is as relaxed as I can get." The others dropped beside her, eager for the rest, and pretended to be snoring. I realized they'd had enough and said, "OK. That's it for today, but as long as you're dreaming, dream of running very fast."

CHAPTER THREE

Braids and Bootie Lock

Team practices went amazingly well. We joked about how tough I was on everyone. They called me "sergeant" and "slave driver." When quarter-miler Chris A'Harrah peeked over the thick eyeglasses that were strapped to her head and called me "Coach Dracula," Evelyn chimed in with "Yeah, she wants our blood." I responded in my best vampire voice: "I don't vant to suck your blood. I vant you to run until you speet eet."

"Oh, yuck" came the groans. But some of them had already had that bloody taste in their mouths that comes after a long, grueling run. They knew I really wasn't kidding.

But by the end of March, as their aching bodies got stronger, they began to admire each other's new muscle definition. Posing in front of the locker-room mirrors, they looked good to themselves. They also felt good when they were able to do all the demanding drills and workouts. They barely noticed that each week the practices were getting harder and longer. I'd added running, jumping, and hopping up and down eighty stadium stairs; box jumps (plyometrics); jogging four-mile laps around the UCLA campus; and water-running in the swimming pool to their regular warm-up, as well as interval training (timed repetitions of 100s, 200s, 300s, etc.).

So far, only Chris and Gayle had problems. Because of a hamstring muscle Chris had pulled in high school, her leg would often cramp up while she was running, causing her to yell out and crumple to the ground. With sweaty blond hair stuck to her face, she looked and felt pathetic. I would stretch out the cramping leg to get her walking again. After her high-school injury, doctors had repeatedly injected her leg with cortisone, but the long needle had further damaged her injured muscle. Now, more than a year later, it was still painful.

As for Gayle, she had cautioned me in our first office visit that she had sickle-cell anemia, a genetic disorder (occurring most often in blacks) causing fever and attacks of pain, mostly in her legs and arms. After reading up on sickle cell, I knew I couldn't push her through hard workouts, and she often was unable to finish our training sessions.

Our first big track meet was at Redlands University, the last weekend in March. As I drove the team out there in the school van, they were like hungry, caged tigers, eager to be turned loose and to test their new bodies.

My "tigers" pounced. Each one nabbed at least one personal record (PR). It seemed that everywhere I looked, the bright yellow-and-teal-blue uniform of UCLA was winning. Then, just as we were getting ready for the 4×100 relay, it started to rain. I thought it might be best to skip the relay. "We should call it quits. You've all done a great job today. We don't need to risk an injury. We've already won the team scoring." (Every athlete earns points for her team based on the place she finishes in her events. The team with the most points wins.)

"We want to run," they said in almost perfect unison. "We can break the UCLA record!"

"Sure you can, but there'll be other meets for record breaking."

Diane Kummer said, "In Chicago we didn't chicken out because of a little rain."

"Yeah, we're tough," said Gayle, having one of her better days. Evelyn was nodding her agreement. I couldn't refuse.

As the leadoff runners were called to their marks, it began to pour. I checked to see that the staggers were properly marked. (Because the track is oval, each lane is a little longer than the lane just inside it. To make the race even, the runners in the longer outside lanes start in front of the others. The staggered starting line insures that each athlete actually runs the same distance around the turns as all the others.) Sharon White, our first runner, got out of the blocks fast, handing the baton to Gayle, who took off in a flurry of long arms and legs. She made up the stagger, passing everyone and bringing "oohs" and "ahs" from the small crowd. Too bad the handoff to Diane was bobbled, leaving her in third. Kicking up mud as she ran, Diane brought us back to second place before she passed the baton to Evelyn. Evelyn started off tenuously, but sixty meters down the straightaway she changed gears. With only one runner to catch, her legs churned faster than ever before. She was battling Rosalyn Bryant, the star American 400-meter record holder from California State Los Angeles. Evelyn began closing the gap. Closer. Closer to Rosalyn Bryant. Then, just ten meters from the tape, Evelyn leaped high into the air. The baton flew out of her hand. For a split second I thought she had misjudged the finish line, but her agonized scream told me immediately that she was seriously hurt.

"Oh my leg, my leg," she wailed, rolling on the muddy track.

"Which leg, Evelyn? Talk to me! Which leg?" I repeated, trying to calm her, having hopped the rail and dashed over to her. She was delirious with pain. We didn't have a team trainer with us, but Cal State L.A. did, and their coach suggested we take Evelyn to her.

There, under the stands, Vicki Vodon had set up her training table. With her strong soothing hands, she was able to diagnose, treat, and bandage the pulled hamstring better than any trainer I'd ever seen. "Evelyn will need careful rehabilitation if her leg is to heal before the Olympic trials in June. Bring her over to Cal State. I'll be glad to treat her and show you some things you can do for her."

Rosalyn Bryant, her hair braided with wooden beads in tight cornrows and still breathing heavily from the relay she'd just won, came to the training bench to wish Evelyn good luck. "Hang in there," said Ros. "Vicki has helped me a lot. She'll help you, too."

Evelyn replied with a barely audible "Thanks. I like your hair."

We all rode back to Los Angeles very quietly.

The next day the UCLA doctor said, "This is a bad pull. Evelyn should not train for at least six weeks." Taking out a syringe, he added, "I'll give her a shot of cortisone to reduce the inflammation."

"Thanks, but no cortisone," I told him, remembering the chronic problems that cortisone injections had caused Chris A'Harrah and other athletes I'd known. I'd once had a shot of the stuff myself, and it only made me hurt and swell more. "I'd

Evelyn's hairstyles changed to match her changing moods.
K. S. Photos   AP/Wide World Photos   Bill Leung

rather Evelyn not have the shot." Seeing the long needle he held, Evelyn nodded her agreement with me. When we left his office, I explained to Evelyn that icing is a better way to stop pain and help healing. "I've always believed that nature's the best healer."

"You're my coach. I'll do what you think is best."

When someone places such confidence in me, it becomes a big responsibility. Her faith made me more determined than ever not to let her down. (Only recently have most doctors stopped injecting cortisone into injured muscles. The experience of athletes usually precedes the knowledge of doctors.)

The UCLA athletic trainer had been told by the team doctor to treat Evelyn with the deep heat of ultrasound. I disagreed and decided to drive Evelyn across town, on my own time, to be treated by Vicki. Vicki confirmed my feelings about ice, showing us a unique way of massaging the muscle with a large chunk of ice (cryotherapy) and then alternating with gradual stretching and resistance called PNF (proprioceptive neuromuscular facilitation). We faithfully followed Vicki's routine, and sooner than anyone predicted, Evelyn was able to start running again.

Shortly after the injury at Redlands, Dr. Judith Holland, the new women's athletic director who had hired me to coach the track-and-field team, called me into her office. "How's Evelyn?" she began.

"She's healing fast. I think she'll be ready to run at collegiate nationals."

"Hmmm. What's this I hear about your neglecting the doctor's orders?"

"Who told you that?"

"Our trainer said that you were taking Evelyn to Cal State L.A."

"That's right. I don't agree with cortisone shots and ultrasound for pulled muscles." After I explained what had happened to Chris years ago, Dr. Holland replied, "You're the coach, but I want to remind you of the tremendous pressure that you put on all of us. This is the first year that women have had financing for intercollegiate programs. Everything we do is being watched critically. You better be right."

"You'll know I'm right when your program produces its first track Olympian this year." (I sounded tougher than I felt.)

By the end of April Evelyn was able to sprint at practice. I decided to let her run a relay in a conference meet at University of California, Santa Barbara. She wasn't too happy about having to run a 400-meter leg of the 1600-meter relay. (The 400-meter, one lap around the track, is the longest sprint race. Sprinters can build up more of the lactic acid that burns in their muscles during a 400-meter run than most marathoners do in twenty-six miles.)

"I can't sprint a four hundred," moaned Evelyn.

"You need the strength that only a competitive

four hundred can give you. Just don't start out too fast. When your bootie [our team name for butt] starts to get tight and you feel like you are running with a five-hundred-pound gorilla on your shoulders, well, you are getting stronger. Right after you finish the race, your bootie will burn, really burn and ache, but try to keep walking. After ten to fifteen minutes the pain will go away.''

"Thanks a lot," Evelyn said with a doubtful look.

Never having run the 400-meter distance before, Evelyn went out too fast in the race. When she grabbed the baton, she trailed two runners. Her racing instincts took over, and before anyone could yell "Slow down," she was five meters in front of both of them.

The Ashford family had driven south from Sacramento to see their own star in Bruin uniform for the first time. They sat in a small crowd that roared as the other, experienced runners began to catch up to Evelyn. She could hear the voices of her teammates screaming. "Pump your arms!" "They're coming!" "Lean, lean for the tape!" But her spent legs were so heavy she could hardly pick them up. She thought she was running on a treadmill, going nowhere.

Evelyn finished second, which to her was *really* nowhere.

Now she was mad, in pain and mad. She had what she called "bootie lock," the burning paralysis she felt in her bootie. Losing made it worse. She dropped on the infield. "Don't touch me," she yelled when I tried to make her get up and start walking off the burning sensation. Her gummy-worm legs would not support her. I held Evelyn around her waist until she could move on her own. "Evelyn, your split [time] was the fastest of all."

"Yeah, but we didn't win!" She spat the words out between quick breaths. Evelyn clearly had the temperament of a champion, though it never was easy getting her to run a 400 after that.

Later, with Evelyn standing beside me, I explained to the Ashfords that I thought Evelyn had a chance to make the Olympic team. "Her injury has been a setback, but everything we do from now on will be to peak her for the trials."

"How is her schoolwork?" asked her father abruptly.

Now I could guess where Evelyn's own abruptness came from. "Her first-quarter grades were passing. I think they'll pick up when she finally decides on a major." I wondered why he'd asked me and not Evelyn.

Mrs. Ashford said, "My daughter respects you. We want to thank you and UCLA for all you are doing for her." She looked like Evelyn—same eyes, cheeks, and smile.

Sergeant Ashford sternly interjected: "See if you can get her to stop reading those Harlequin romances, and if you have any problems with Evelyn, just let me know."

"Thank you, but Evelyn is no problem," I replied, and the Ashfords were off, piling their other children into the family car.

CHAPTER FOUR

Other Coaches

"My men have a job to do," grumped Jim Bush, head coach of the UCLA men's track-and-field team. "I don't want your women trying to distract them while we're out here training."

"I don't want your guys distracting my team either," I snapped back. "We'll be working just as intensely as you." Standing up to Coach Bush was not easy. He was one of the most successful and respected college coaches, and I'd adapted some of his innovations for coaching runners into my own program.

Love affairs did spring up between some of the men and women on the two teams, but these affairs were never allowed to interfere with practices at Drake Stadium. For example, one day I saw Chris A'Harrah sneaking away with Coach Bush's new quarter-miler, Benny Miles. I surprised them so quickly, they accused me of having eyes in the back of my head.

Within a few weeks Coach Bush realized how serious we were about training, and he grew to be one of our greatest supporters. Other coaches, however, were becoming openly critical of my coaching methods. "Aren't you going to do something about Ashford's low arms and exaggerated forward lean?" asked Tom Tellez, one of the UCLA assistant men's coaches who had tried to work with Evelyn before I'd been hired. "She runs too much like a girl."

"Evelyn has the greatest natural gift that I have ever seen. Trying to change her would be like trying to teach a cheetah how to run."

"According to the laws of physics as they relate to the biomechanics of running, Evelyn's wasting a great deal of motion," insisted the academic Tellez.

Women of my generation and earlier had been coached by men who believed that techniques developed for men were the only road to success. I had decided that women should be coached differently from men. "Coach, compared to men we have greater stamina but weaker upper bodies and wider hips. It takes us longer to make gains in strength, so our training progressions must be more patient. What you see now as flaws in Evelyn's technique will improve as she gets stronger. Take the way her feet whip around with each step. You'll see that with the proper training, the whip can become an advantage for her."

A greater threat to my team was a local club coach whom I'll call Tyrone Thompson. (I have changed his name.) Tyrone had applied for my job at UCLA. In his disappointment over not being offered the job, he set out to undermine my program. He considered himself quite the ladies' man in his unbuttoned sports shirt and numerous gold chains. But I thought if he tied a scarf around his head, he'd look like a pirate from a nearby Hollywood set. Often lurking around our campus, he stopped Evelyn one day. "You can be the best sprinter of all time, but only if I teach you my secrets of running. Connolly doesn't know what she's doing."

"Really?"

"Why don't you come practice with my team? You should be coached by one of your own people."

"I'll think about it," said Evelyn, now anxious to get away.

When I found out about her encounter with Tyrone, I cautioned her and the rest of my team to resist him. "He's exploited a lot of athletes. Remember how Pinocchio was lured to Pleasure Island by the fox? Well, Tyrone Thompson's athletes end up donkeys, just like the stupid boys who went with the fox."

Fortunately Evelyn listened to her own personal Jiminy Cricket. She had a very strong conscience thanks to her parents and strict grandmother.

Tyrone wasn't the only coach who tried to entice Evelyn away. But the growing prestige of our team, the rapport between Evelyn and myself, and her improving speed, not to mention her father's insistence, kept Evelyn from leaving UCLA.

The major meet for the UCLA team in 1976 was the Women's National Collegiate Championships in Kansas to be held May 13–15. My son Adam was only eight months old, and because I was still breast-feeding him, I would have to take him with us on the week-long trip. Harold would stay at home with my ten-year-old son Bradley, and Harold's four children from his first marriage: Mark, fifteen; twins Jimmy and Merja, twelve; and Nina, ten. Taking Adam to the championships was good for another reason: Critics of women's athletics who claimed that women coaches (and athletes) were too masculine could see that I was a caring mother as well as a tough coach.

During our flight to Kansas my athletes took turns holding and playing with Adam until he threw up his dinner all over Diane Kummer's freshly shampooed hair. Diane got up good-naturedly and asked the stewardess for a damp cloth while the rest of the girls laughed. Karin hollered, "Way to go, Adam. You know how to pick the pretty girls."

In Kansas I gave rival coaches more reasons to criticize me, and they didn't hesitate to tell Dr. Holland, who later reported their comments to me. One such charge was that I was stupid for not entering a 4×100 relay, that I'd thrown away points that they knew we could have won. After all, hadn't Evelyn already placed second in the 100 meters? And Gayle sixth? And Diane eighth? UCLA could easily have won ten first-place points with this many top sprinters on its team. These same coaches also scolded me for taking Karin out of the javelin competition before her final two throws.

"Who does Pat Connolly think she is? Her athletes are too pampered."

I had excellent reasons for both of these decisions. The upcoming Olympic trials were just four weeks away (June 19–27). If any of my athletes had been injured by running too many races, they might never have had another Olympic opportunity. They'd worked hard all winter and spring just to qualify for the trials. And they'd already broken the school relay records. Why make them run yet another relay? And as for Karin Smith, I yanked her out of her competition in the pouring rain, where she might have slipped or gotten chilled and then sick. She'd already won the javelin event with her first four throws. Why take more chances?

Yes, I was putting their individual Olympic hopes ahead of a UCLA team victory in Kansas (we finished in eighth place), but in the process I was scoring valuable points with my own athletes who wanted to be Olympians more than anything else.

The last chance for a tune-up race before the

Olympic trials was the Senior and Junior National Championships, to be held at Drake Stadium. I chose to enter Evelyn, who had just turned nineteen that April, in the junior race. There she wouldn't have to face Chandra and Brenda, who were entered in the senior division. I'd hoped Evelyn would be able to win easily and go to the trials with increased confidence.

She spent the morning of her race taking her final exam in sociology and arrived at the track with barely enough time to warm up. She seemed weary and her mind far away. To shake her out of her lethargy, I said, "The favorites are being upset by nobodies. The last thing you want to do is fall asleep and be surprised, so wake up or you'll end up in second place!"

Not even the starter's gun awoke Evelyn. Her start, the weakest part of her race, was wobbly. She was still in second at sixty meters, where I expected her to change gears and accelerate ahead to win.

Her gears were stuck and she finished where she started, in second.

I went down to console Evelyn. "I don't have it! I'll never make the team." She was crying and leaving the stadium without warming down.

Dragging her by one arm, I got her to jog slowly with me. "You're drained from exams but I made a mistake too." Evelyn looked at me with an expression that clearly said, "What are you talking about?"

"Remember how we discussed the need for a positive mental attitude before a race? I sent you out there with negative statements, like 'you'll end up in second place.' You did what I said. I'll never make that mistake again. Don't take this loss too seriously. You have ten days before the trials, with no books or classes to worry about. Let me do the worrying; you do the running and have fun."

School was out for my children as well as for my athletes, and I decided to take Adam and Bradley with me to the trials in Eugene, Oregon. Harold wanted to see the trials too, but he had to teach summer school and watch the other kids. We'd travel in our family's huge Ford camper that looked like a covered wagon. There was room for my mother and teenage sister, Elizabeth (baby-sitters!), and for Ed Parker, who'd been my own coach when I'd competed in three Olympic trials and games. Now that I was a coach myself, I appreciated more than ever what he'd done for me. We took turns driving while he listened to my ideas about coaching. His support felt wonderful after the criticism I'd taken from others.

We all settled down in a motel near the University of Oregon track. The weather looked great as I drove to the airport to pick up my athletes. But

Eugene was a dangerous place for anyone who was allergic to the numerous pollens in the air. Having no allergies myself, I didn't realize the damage they could do until both Evelyn and Karin got off the plane and started a sneezing contest. At first I thought they were teasing, but as their eyes, ears, and noses turned red, I knew we were in trouble. Other coaches suggested they take antihistamines, but I didn't let my athletes take them for two reasons. First, I didn't know what effect the drugs might have on their performances, for we'd never tried them before. Second (and more important), some antihistamines contained substances that were banned by the Olympic Committee.

From my first days as an athlete and then as a coach, I'd been very strict about playing by the rules, so in Eugene, Karin and Evelyn took no antihistamines. Instead they both stayed in the motel most of the time, where air conditioners filtered the pollen. They stretched and exercised inside. Karin visited the rooms of friends from other teams, but Evelyn didn't know many people and she hung out with my family. I put a mattress on the floor of my room, and would give Evelyn rub downs and stretches (the PNF we had learned from Vicki) while Adam crawled all over us wanting to play, biting Evelyn's toes and tickling her feet until my mother took him away.

Evelyn laughed, asking, "Is that part of the treatment?" Being the oldest of five kids and having to travel so much ever since she'd been a youngster, Evelyn was able to adapt to almost anything. Now faced with the most important races of her life, her temperament remained sunny, at least away from the track.

Karin Smith made the Olympic team easily. She chucked her javelin 187 feet 9 inches for third place in the competition, then bounced around the field in her red handkerchief, blue-and-gold Bruin uniform, and bright-green shoes. Finally she climbed into the grandstands to hug everyone she knew.

Evelyn had just completed her warm-up for the quarterfinal when she heard Karin's success being announced. She looked at me excitedly, and I said, "Tomorrow after the one-hundred final you'll be the next Bruin on the team."

Evelyn qualified easily in the first two rounds. The next day, after placing second to Chandra in the semifinal, the tension started to mount. "Karin is saving a place for you on the Olympic team, so go get it." Those were the last words Evelyn heard before the gun. At the start of her final race she became more inwardly focused than I had ever seen her.

When I noticed that one of her competitors had mistakenly reversed the position of Evelyn's foot pedals, which could cause her to stumble or fall as she began the race, I yelled, "Fix your blocks!" But Evelyn was in another world. The blocks stayed wrong. I barely had time to run around to the other side of the track, where I could see the race and the finish line. The crack of the gun startled me. Then I panicked. I couldn't find Evelyn, who was obscured in the middle of the pack. At fifty meters I could see she had no chance to win. Brenda and Chandra were too far in front.

Evelyn had to be at least third to make the team. I didn't yell aloud, but my insides were screaming, "You've got to want it more than they do."

At seventy meters—yeah! Evelyn found the same gear that she had used at Redlands but never since then because of her injury. She had the pure speed to pull ahead of the pack and almost catch the two leaders. Third place! She did it! She was an Olympian with a new UCLA record and a time faster than Wilma Rudolph had ever run, 11.26. I stood in the stands savoring the moment, letting the tears of relief and joy flood my face. Evelyn was stunned. When she heard her name announced, she leaped so high in the air, she astonished herself and the happy crowd who were applauding the three new Olympians. Karin made her way to Evelyn's side saying, "Welcome to the U.S. Olympic team." She herself had been a member only a day longer than her teammate.

Now they would go to live at the U.S. Olympic Team Camp at Lake Placid, a small town in upstate New York. Team policy would not allow me to stay at the camp and work with them. I knew from my own Olympic Camp experiences that this month could be a huge, wonderful party beginning with new clothes (USA uniforms) and new friends and ending with banquets and dances. I also knew that without their own coaches to guide them, many young athletes would skip their workouts. I told Evelyn and Karin to phone me collect if they had camp problems, yet I knew Evelyn said so little, it would be hard to really know what was going on without being able to see her expressions.

I gave Evelyn the training schedule I'd prepared and said to both of them, "You are capable of achieving personal records in Montreal. I don't care what place you take in your events, but I do expect PR's from each of you."

Evelyn's Olympic coach would be Brooks Johnson. I'd never heard of him, but I spoke with him and got his assurance that he wouldn't change anything in Evelyn's technique. I later learned from both Evelyn and Johnson himself that she gave him no trouble at camp. It wasn't her nature to be contrary, and she easily became his favorite. Johnson explained that the prima-donna sprinters from Tennessee State tried to make Evelyn look bad at relay practice by varying their speed during the baton exchange. (As a result the USA relay team that should have won a medal wasn't even in the Olympic 4×100 final, a clear sign of poor leadership.)

I hated being at home and having to watch Evelyn's 100-meter final on TV. I wanted to be able to study her face and body movements as she warmed up. When she did take her mark, I could see that Johnson had changed her start. As Evelyn got out of the blocks, dead last, I jumped out of the chair yelling so furiously at Johnson that Harold had to tell me where she finished.

"It looks like she's fifth," he said.

The announcer confirmed her fifth place and her time of 11.24—a new personal record that was amazing, since her changed start was atrocious! She was the first American finisher, ahead of Chandra, who was sixth. (Brenda had been injured and was not in the final.)

From watching the replay of the finish, I knew Evelyn would have medaled if only her start had been left alone. Her acceleration in the final forty meters was incredible, faster than that of Annegret Richter, the winner, who had set a new world record in the semis of 11.01 seconds.

"Evelyn will be the next great sprinter, if other coaches will leave her alone," I told Harold, who replied, "Talent isn't everything. A lot can happen. But you've done a good job with her, coach."

CHAPTER FIVE

No Drugs for Us

When I picked Evelyn up at Los Angeles International Airport, she handed me a present from Montreal, a live Canadian maple tree with instructions for planting. (A maple leaf appears on the Canadian flag and saplings had been presented to all of the finalists.) "What a great gift. I'll plant this in my front yard tomorrow. It will be our Olympic tree.

"Well, what did you think? Were the Games worth all the work?"

"Oh, yes. It was like being a part of the biggest sparkling party you can imagine. It sparkled, everything just sparkled." Evelyn was so excited that for once she kept on talking.

As she told me her impressions, I remembered my first Olympic Games. I was still sixteen, and there I was, marching in the front row of the USA team with then-famous athletes like Wilma Rudolph, Donna de Varona, Rafer Johnson, Jerry West, and Cassius Clay (Muhammad Ali). It was like we were the center of the universe. The teams were introduced, speeches were made, and then we took the Athlete's Oath: "The important thing in the Olympic Games is not to win but to take part, the important thing in life is not the triumph but the struggle." Just looking at the wide-eyed wonder on Evelyn's face gave me that feeling all over again. We'd both delighted in the rainbow of national flags that represented the participating countries and their people who stood beside us on the infield in their colorful native costumes and uniforms. We'd loved the trumpet fanfares and orchestras that scored the Olympic pageant like an opera. Remembering the pigeons that were released as a symbol of peace, I said, "I hope the pigeons were better behaved in Montreal than the pigeons in Rome."

Evelyn smiled. "Luckily our team wasn't standing under the heaviest barrage. I think the pigeons got some East Germans, though."

"How did you feel when the torch was lit?"

"It made me jittery when I realized that my race would become a permanent part of Olympic history."

I then told Evelyn that Ed Temple, coach of the Women's Olympic track-and-field team in 1960, 1964, and 1968, had given the pigeons their highest compliment. He'd said, "But shoot, when the pigeons fly, you betta be ready!"

Evelyn had been ready, with her fastest time ever.

Modupe Oshikoya from Nigeria was not as lucky as Evelyn or as Karin, who'd placed eighth. Modupe had been kept from competing in the '76 Games because her own country, as well as other African nations, had not sent teams to Montreal. Instead they had chosen to boycott the Olympics as a way of making a statement against the racial laws (apartheid) in South Africa. Politics, having nothing to do with sport, had robbed Modupe and her fellow Africans of their chance to be in Olympic history books. Now, in the fall of 1976, Modupe sat in my office, telling me how impressed she'd been by Evelyn's and Karin's performances and asking me for an athletic scholarship.

I knew Modupe was a fine pentathlete (the pentathlon is five events: 100-meter hurdles, shot put, high jump, long jump, and 200-meter dash, scored on the basis of performance in each event) who'd competed in the Munich Olympics as a teenager. Of course I wanted her on our team. We could use another hurdler, and I definitely needed a long jumper, because Diane Kummer had returned to Chicago to get married. (I hated to lose her but I never argued with a diamond ring!) Modupe's speed would also be an asset on our relay teams. She might even prove to be a team leader.

The team took to "Dupe" (pronounced Do-Pay) right away. They were inspired by her conscientious approach to schoolwork and to training. They tried hard to get Dupe to understand and laugh at their jokes. When they yelled encouragement to her as she ran her time trials, they called her "MoMo." One day at practice Jan Lester, our hurdler who looked like a cheerleader, got so excited seeing Dupe on her way to a PR that she didn't even realize what she was yelling: "Go, Doo Doo! Go, Doo Doo!"

It was the team's first autumn together, the time when the body must be prepared for the stresses of spring and summer competitions. In my opening lecture to the team at Drake Stadium, I reminded them that American women athletes had for too long been considered flabby and lackadaisical about competition.

"We're going to change that image," I insisted. "We'll be in better shape than the men's football team."

"Who do you think we are, East Germans?" asked Jan. She'd watched East Germany (Deutsche Demotratische Republik, or DDR) sweep many Olympic events, and set world records while they were at it.

I fastened my eyes on my team. "You are going to be better than East Germans!"

"Oh, sure," moaned the cynics.

"How can we compete with them without taking

the same drugs they do?" Karin asked. She'd learned from her new friends in Montreal about the male hormones that Eastern European women were taking to build their strength.

For a moment I let Karin's question hang in the air while I thought about my own introduction to steroids. I decided it would be helpful to tell the team about my experience. Gathering them around me on the grass, I began. "In 1960 when I first started competing, some of the winners were men disguised as women."

"You gotta be kidding," cried Gina Hendy, an A-student sprinter from northern California.

"It's true, though I didn't know it at the time. Because those athletes' hard, well-defined muscles and thickened facial hair looked unfeminine, my grandmother and others were worried that I would become like a man if I competed in track-and-field. I was surprised to hear the deep male voices of some of my competitors. Olympic officials became so alarmed by this, they devised a test to certify that all competitors in women's events were truly women. Before we were allowed to compete we were given what I called the 'peek-and-poke' test. Official doctors examined us for breasts, and by poking around our genitals, they made sure we didn't have a penis or testicles. It was humiliating!"

"Revolting!" Jan exclaimed.

"We submitted only because we wanted the competition to be fair. A few years later it was learned that some who were certified women shouldn't have been. At birth, through an unfortunate mix-up of nature, these women had inherited a male chromosome that might give them an unfair advantage. Officials decided to change the test from a physical examination to a chromosome test. This was great news. Now all we had to do was let a lab technician scrape some cells from the insides of our mouths and then examine the cells with a microscope. Under magnification, female sex chromatin, or the Barr body, looks like a little tennis racket on the cell nucleus. Those of us with this chromatin were certified as women. The ones without the Barr body were not certified, and were subjected to more stringent testing. This procedure would now eliminate all competitors who had malelike advantages."

That's more like it," interjected high jumper Chris Remmling.

"You can imagine how we kidded each other at being 'card-carrying women,' but at least we didn't have to take the peek-and-poke test anymore." Then, with a mischievous grin, I said, "I believe Karin, Evelyn, Modupe, Debbie, Kathy, and Cindy are all card-carrying women." I was interrupted by raucous applause. "Don't forget that at the time of my first test in 1967, I was a mother, yet I still had to be certified. The rest of you will be certified women when you make an international team. Ah, such motivation!"

Cindy wondered aloud, "What do the men have to do to prove they are men?"

"Nothing. Maybe you want to be the official male certifier?"

"Oh no, not me!"

Evelyn blurted out, "I wouldn't mind certifying some of the men I met on the Olympic team." Now there were catcalls and echoes of "Who? Who?"

"So what does this have to do with steroids?" asked Dupe.

Getting serious again, I explained, "With the introduction of the chromosome test we women thought at last the competition would be fair. But

Pat Winslow-Connolly winning the pentathlon and 200m in the Pan American Games just after passing the "peek-&-poke" test.

starting around the time of the 1968 Olympics, we had a new problem. Certain female-certified European women were being given male hormones as part of their training routine, and these women were leading the parade to the victory stands. At first I couldn't believe that women would take drugs to improve their performances, especially since steroids were thought to be dangerous to good health. But unnatural improvements in many of the world's track-and-field records could hardly be explained otherwise. Too rapidly to be considered normal progress, the discus record went from under two hundred feet to over two hundred and twenty feet!"

"So did the javelin and the long jump," offered Karin.

"I didn't learn about steroids until 1970. When I did, I felt cheated and terribly sad for women. Natural women had never had a chance to compete only against other natural women, and at last when we thought things would be fair, the growing use of male hormones by female athletes took that chance from us. I was devastated by this news. Improving my own records was the most important reward of my career. If I used drugs, I would never know if my improvement was due to my own ability or to miracles of the laboratory." (Some of the athletes had heard this before, but I repeated it for the new members.)

With all eyes on me I was nearing the end of

my story. "In the spring of 1972 I was the best American pentathlete. I'd been ranked third in the world. As the Olympic trials approached, a certain coach began pushing me to take steroids, claiming that without them I had no chance to win an Olympic medal. I argued with him, flat out refusing his offer to get steroids for me. The next time he brought up the subject, I quit track—quit for good, screaming that if I had to take male hormones to be up there among the world's best, well, he and the rest of the cheaters could go to hell."

Cindy broke the silence that followed. "How do you expect us to beat the European women if you weren't able to do it without drugs?"

"Because I've devised a better training program for you. I believe my program will, given enough time, get a gifted and determined athlete into such fine shape she won't need the shortcut that drugs provide. Drugs are risky. They've been banned, so you'd be cheating to use them. And worse, they could change you in ways you'd truly end up hating."

"Like what?"

"You'd stop menstruating, for example."

"I wouldn't care about that." Cindy was talking and the rest were nodding in agreement.

"You'd care when the hair on your face got so thick you had to shave and when you got terrible acne and your voice dropped so low people thought you were a man when they heard you on the phone. And, do you really want to run an increased risk of getting cancer?

"I lost heart in 1972, but I've got it back from working with this team. You have inspired me, and I'll share my newfound strength with anyone who wants to work. I believe women don't need male hormones to be good athletes, and I've put together a program to prove it."

My team didn't complain about the long workouts after that.

CHAPTER SIX

Weights, Waves, and Dirty Dishes

Some people think that an athletic scholarship provides a free ride through college. Not so. Many athletes have to hold down part-time jobs as well as go to class, do their homework, and attend every practice and game. They often have tons of make-up work from classes missed while they travel to competitions. My extra demands on the team, especially the hour-long sessions in the weight-training room, didn't make their college life much easier.

At that time very few women had been exposed to pumping iron. I had not done much lifting as an athlete myself, but research had proved that women's performances improved as their muscles grew stronger.

"You vill be strong!" I encouraged my athletes in a phony German accent.

Too tired to respond, they looked at me as if to say, "Get off it." But they kept up their circuit of exercises. Each athlete in turn moved from station to station, working her stomach (abdominal) muscles, quadriceps, hamstrings, hip flexors, back, shoulders, feet, triceps, lower legs, chest, and bootie. By their third week of weights everyone could repeat the eleven stations twice in one training session. When each athlete was finally able to complete the circuit three times, I began to increase the amount of weight she used.

"When does this stop? We're racehorses, not packhorses, ya know," groaned Debbie.

Evelyn surprised me by being one of the weakest on the team. Weighing 115 pounds, she could bench press only 40 pounds. (Women athletes should be able to bench at least their own body weight.) I took Evelyn's weakness as a good sign. If she could run as fast as she had in Montreal as a weakling, I could expect real improvement in her times as she got stronger.

She didn't mind the weight work as much as the long, long runs I made my sprinters do that fall of 1976. I coaxed Evelyn along when she told me, "My feet are asleep. They're needles and pins." I had her try different pairs of shoes over the next few runs, but that didn't make a difference.

"Do I really have to run three miles?" she'd ask pleadingly, "My calves are almost numb."

"Have you ever been tested for sickle-cell anemia?"

"No, but nobody in my family has ever had that problem."

Too afraid to find out for sure if she really had sickle cell, I didn't insist on her getting tested right away. Instead I stayed up nights reading scientific journals and finally found an article that had a possible explanation for Evelyn's dislike of distance running. Each individual inherits two different kinds of fibers that make up each muscle: the first, slow-twitch fibers that carry lots of oxygen allowing an athlete to go for long, slow runs with comfort; and the second, fast-twitch fibers that enable an athlete to react quickly, jump high, and run fast. These fast-twitch fibers create quick bursts of power but have limited capacity to carry oxygen.

Could it be that Evelyn's muscles were made up mostly of fast-twitch fibers? Wasn't her standing vertical jump the highest on the team? And her short sprint the fastest? She must be a "pure" sprinter, with comparatively few slow-twitch fibers to carry enough oxygen to run the longer distances. Her feet and calves fell asleep through no fault of her own nor of my training program: Her fast-twitch fibers must be inherited.

I dropped her weekly distance work to a mile per session until her time improved to under 6:30 minutes and her feet stayed "awake." Over the next few years she gradually was able to work her way back up to three- and even four-mile runs.

For variety we occasionally warmed up with informal soccer games or Frisbee football but Evelyn was not the star of anything that required a ball. She was practically blind without her contact lenses, and even with them her vision was poor. We also trained at Venice Beach some days. These training sessions were as serious as the ones at Drake Stadium, and I didn't let my athletes wiggle out of them, not even in horrible weather.

"Let's go to the movies," Evelyn begged one rainy Saturday in January of 1977 after she and the others got soaked just piling into my van.

Sunset Boulevard was flooded. We inched along. After a few miles the van's brakes were wet and didn't work well. The team sat silently while I thought of turning around, of going back home and baking cookies for my children. Then I thought about winning—winning races, high jumps, long jumps, discus and javelin throws, relays—and becoming the best college team in America. I kept driving. The trip was so tense that when we finally made it, the athletes jumped up and down on the sand, whooping in relief. I kept them moving so they wouldn't get cold. I tried to run with them, but I couldn't keep their pace. Even in a downpour they were now too fast for me.

Trash cans dotted the beach about 120 yards apart. The team had to sprint to the first can, then jog to the next, then sprint to the next, and so on until they reached the rocks at the end of that beach. Then they turned around and jogged all the way back. After repeating the sprint-jog three times, I had them bound with long, leaping strides to the first can and then walk back at a fast pace, dragging their toes and kicking sand up in front of them. The added resistance of the sand was making their feet sore, so I said, "Just one more drill—high knee fifty meters through the surf."

"No way, not me," exclaimed Evelyn, whose drenched and matted hair made her look like a drowning victim. "I can't swim."

"We can't either." Evelyn's teammates joined in the rebellion, but I knew most of them had graduated from California high schools, which require each student to pass a swimming test in order to earn a diploma.

"You'll be in water only up to your hips. And you're all strong enough not to be knocked down by a wave. Come on, I'll go with you. This is the last drill. Afterward I'll take you all to my house and fix breakfast." I grabbed Evelyn and Modupe by the hand and walked them to the water; it didn't feel cold because we were already wet. "If you lose your balance, grab me. I'm a strong swimmer."

Surrounded by frothy surf, Evelyn and Modupe began running with exaggerated high-knee lifts so that their feet cleared the water. At first I held their hands, but soon they let go for better balance. After six 50-yard repeats they were exhausted, yet not too far gone to douse me in the salty water. We changed to dry clothes at the Connolly-family house, which was one mile inland from Venice Beach. For breakfast I made wheat-germ pancakes and hot cinnamon apple cider.

The team members were overcoming their fears of hard work and of high surf. A feeling of invincibility crept over our warming, tired bones.

The very next Monday I was called to the office of the UCLA women's athletic director, Judith Holland. She came right to the point: Evelyn and Karin were being placed on academic probation. If their grades didn't improve, they wouldn't be allowed to compete in the spring track meets. Dr. Holland went on to tell me there had been complaints that my athletes were so tired from their workouts that they couldn't study.

"Who's complaining?"

"I promised confidentiality."

"We can't win the Nationals this year without hard work." In my mind's eye I glimpsed Evelyn's matted hair and Karin's aching back and sore knees. I sank down in the chair in front of Holland's desk. "I'll try to lighten up their training load." Student-athletes cannot train as hard as other athletes. Was I guilty of pressing too hard to find their limits?

I decided to see Evelyn before I went home. When I called her dorm, one of her roommates said she was working in the campus cafeteria, known as the Tree House. I didn't believe it. Evelyn hadn't mentioned a job. When I entered the Tree House to find not only Evelyn, but Karin as well, rushing from table to table with trays of dirty dishes, my heart sank. They were both shocked to see me.

"We're goners," Karin whispered to Evelyn. Evelyn still wasn't a talker, but I could read her body language and especially her eyes, which asked, "How did you find out?"

"When will you be finished?" I asked them.

"In half an hour," they said in unison.

"I'll get a salad and wait for you."

Eating alone in a corner, I thought about Evelyn's grant-in-aid. It paid for her tuition, her room, and board but not for her books, clothes, toothpaste, shampoo, or for the movies she loved seeing on weekends. Such spending money came from her parents, who had four younger children to support. Apparently she needed this job that was also stealing her time from studying.

Rather than have Evelyn and Karin wear themselves out, I could have found a wealthy UCLA alumnus to give them all the spending money they needed. But collegiate rules prevented them and all other athletes playing on college teams from accepting gifts from alumni, coaches, or anyone except parents or guardians. Evelyn and Karin were on the verge of flunking out of school because of that rule. If they flunked, they'd lose this opportunity for an education. They would have no coach, no trainer, no equipment, no travel budget. They would probably have to work at a low-paying job just to feed and house themselves.

"I know how hard it is not to have money in your pockets," I began when they joined me at my table. "But you've taken on too much. Dr. Holland informs me that your grades are suffering."

They looked at each other like kids who had been caught with their hands in the cookie jar.

"You must quit these jobs and make appointments with tutors for your difficult classes. I'll lighten up on your workouts so that you won't be too tired to study. By sacrificing now, your empty pockets will fill up much later when you have your education and can get good jobs."

"I know I want to run, but I don't know why I want a college degree," Evelyn said, opening up.

"Don't you have career goals?"

"Not really. There isn't a major here at UCLA that interests me."

"Isn't your major sociology?"

"Only because I couldn't get into the School of Dance."

"Dance?" I couldn't recall Evelyn even tapping her toes to the music other team members would blast on trips.

"My grandmother was so strict, she wouldn't let us have any music in the house. I've often dreamed of being a dancer."

"Have you ever taken lessons?"

"No. But isn't that what school is for, to teach me?"

"UCLA's Department of Dance is one of the most prestigious in the country. They are choosy. Students who apply must already be experienced dancers."

"Well, there goes that dream. I guess I'm stuck in sociology," said a dejected Evelyn. The only other subjects that interested her were sewing and homemaking, but UCLA had no home-economics major.

Karin's problem with her grades stemmed from not having a goal beyond being the best javelin thrower in the world. She would have liked to be paid at track meets instead of being handed a trophy that was doomed to gather dust on a shelf. Unfortunately, in 1977, American women could not earn a living throwing the javelin or running races.

CHAPTER SEVEN

Double Double

Evelyn's quicksilver days of being uncatchable on the track were about to begin. She would not lose a single race during the 1977 collegiate season.

That season, however, almost took place without her, and not because of her poor grades. With the help of tutors she managed to raise her grade-point average. But then one Monday she failed to show up for practice. I noticed hushed conversations among my athletes that afternoon. When she wasn't there on Tuesday, I asked if anyone knew why Evelyn wasn't at practice. My athletes sheepishly shook their heads.

When she was still missing on Friday, I said in a deliberate, low voice, "Since you seem to know what is going on but don't want to tell me, make certain that Evelyn gets this message: If she's not at practice on Monday with a very good excuse, she will not remain a member of this team."

Her teammates knew I meant it. I'd already kicked two athletes off the team for being late, missing practices, and profanely criticizing the new obstacle course I'd introduced to our training program. Dr. Holland had been surprised that I'd sent two black athletes packing. She'd worried about a possible charge of racism, but I'd told her, "I don't care what color they are. If they're not at practice, they are not on my team. My stopwatch and tape measure don't see color, only performance." Dr. Holland nervously agreed to support my decision.

Sunday morning I was awakened by the phone. "This is Evelyn. I'll be at practice tomorrow."

"Are you in trouble? What's happening?" I asked.

"I went with my boyfriend to San Jacinto. He had some problems and we couldn't get back to campus." Evelyn paused and then went into the details of her misadventures. I forgave the missed practices. "I'll see you tomorrow," she said, seeming embarrassed about having shared her private troubles with me.

On Monday, seated in my office, Evelyn was the picture of contrition. I told her, "You can be to sprinting what Beethoven is to music, what Michelangelo is to art. But without the determination to reach your goals you'll falter as you did last week. You'll end up like other talented losers. Nowhere."

She sat perfectly still.

"Do you really want to be the best?"

Evelyn said a quiet "Yes," but resolve shone in her eyes.

UCLA was hosting the women's National Collegiate Championships in May 1977. To compete on the familiar track of Drake Stadium would be an advantage for my team but would also mean many extra hours of work for me as meet director. Numerous phone calls had to be made, officials arranged, and sponsors lined up; meet information packets, programs, and schedules had to be written; and the entries had to be seeded as they came in. I rarely got home from my office until very late. My husband and children complained they didn't see enough of me. It seemed there was always a pile of laundry blocking my way out the door, and I couldn't afford help with cooking, cleaning, and other housework because my salary was so low: $5,000 for the year (compared with the more than $30,000 paid to the men's track coach). Harold's meager teacher's salary and my own barely supported our family of eight.

Vicki Vodon also worked around the clock as the new athletic trainer for the team. I'd persuaded Dr. Holland to offer her the job, and now Vicki made it her goal to get everyone healthy and ready for the Nationals. We expected our toughest competition to come from Prairie View University, California State at Los Angeles, and especially from California State at Northridge, which was coached by the very man who'd urged me to take steroids, way back when I was training for the '72 Olympics. Needless to say we were looking forward to beating Northridge.

Every member of our team would be trying to score as many points as possible. Modupe Oshikoya, for example, would compete in the high jump, long jump, hurdles, and relays. Half milers Debbie Roberson and Kathy Weston would each have seven races counting heats, and Evelyn would be running in five events: the 100 meters, the 200 meters, the 4×100 relay, and the 200 leg on the 800-meter medley relay, and a tough 400 on the 1600 relay. With the heats she'd be going to the starting line *nine times in three days.* On the first day Evelyn moved through her preliminary rounds with ease. The second day was tougher as she barely edged Andrea Lynch in the 100-meter final (Andrea had been an Olympian in '76 representing Great Britain). Later that day Evelyn stunned everyone by running 22.2 for her 200-meter leg of the medley relay (which consists of 200–100–100–400), putting her team so far out in front that the race was virtually over before her other three teammates had even gotten the baton. Her time was an unofficial world record. (A time that is run as part of a relay team is not accepted as a record.) Then, even though she ran easily the third day in the 200-meter final to save her sore legs for the relays, she still won in the fastest time of her life, almost breaking Cheeseborough's American record.

Both of her relay teams were victorious and set college records. All together she'd scored 24.5 points to help us cinch the team title.

Drake Stadium had never seen such a celebration. Lisa Vogelsang, our discus champion, and Karin, who won the javelin, along with my other delirious athletes, threatened to throw me into the steeple-chase water jump as they'd seen the men's team do in previous years; but because there is no steeple-chase competition at women's track meets, the jump was empty and I pleaded for mercy as they carried me on their shoulders. Even Dr. Holland, who was normally unemotional, came up and gave me a con-gratulatory hug. I would have liked to go out on the town celebrating with my champions, but I'd promised my family I'd be home as soon as the meet was over. I still count that team victory as one of the most significant of my career, not to mention the success of having staged a great Na-tional Championships. But I was afraid to let myself have fun; I felt guilty having taken so much time from my family with so little income to show for it.

Just two weeks after those Collegiate Champion-ships, Evelyn won the 100 with an 11.14 PR and the 200 at the National Outdoor Championships.

Her time of 22.62 for the 200-meter dash established a new American record. Just as I'd promised, she'd shown Brenda and Chandra her behind. What's more, she'd completed a very rare "double double": winning two races at Collegiate Nationals and the same two distances at the National Outdoor Championships. No longer could anyone doubt that Evelyn Ashford was America's fastest female runner.

Her training continued to go well until Evelyn learned that Marlies Oelsner, an East German, had set a new world record in the 100 meter—10.88! The track world was agog. Many experts had long believed that women would never run the hundred under eleven seconds. As for me, I was certain that breaking the eleven-second barrier lay within Evelyn's reach. I had even secretly hoped she would be the first woman to do it.

She threw her spikes to the ground when I told her about Marlies. "She didn't break it, she smashed it. That's it for me." Evelyn rarely wore makeup, not even lipstick, and her hair was simply braided. She looked young and vulnerable.

"You'll run faster than that," I predicted.

"No way!"

"Remember, Evelyn, after your bad start in Montreal, you came from behind Marlies to beat her by more than a meter? She can't be any better than you are . . . just more advanced in her training." But even to myself I wasn't sure what their training methods were. How could chunky Marlies with her choppy stride be faster than Evelyn? The East German's secret sports training camp in Leipzig was off limits to foreign visitors. (Although there is no direct evidence that Marlies enhanced her performance with drugs, it has since been reported by former DDR coaches and athletes that drugs were being tested on some of their athletes.) But I didn't want to offer Evelyn or the other athletes who were standing there an excuse that could lead to mediocre performances.

"I like the two hundred better anyway," mumbled Evelyn, whose slow start from the blocks made the shorter race more difficult for her. She jogged out of Drake in a huff, clearly upset.

To athletes and coaches world records are sacred things. Hard to achieve and scrutinized by several teams of officials, those little black numbers in a record book are the biggest goal, as well as the toughest psychological barrier, in sports. Unlike a competitor you can see in your race, the world record sits there known but intangible. Everyone wants the record to have his or her name on it, yet just that fact makes it seem impossible. Rare is the athlete who predicts and then actually breaks a world record—especially in the sprints, where the lowering of records seems to be near its limit. (It had been nine years since the world record in the men's 100 meters had been set, and literally dozens of incredibly fast men had tried to break it. It wasn't until 1983—fifteen years after the setting of the record—that Calvin Smith lowered that men's mark from 9.95 to 9.93.) In 1977 Evelyn couldn't help but wonder if 10.88 would stand for nine years, or possibly forever.

By winning at the National Outdoor Championships Evelyn had qualified for the U.S. team's summer trip to Europe. But our happiness at her tremendous improvements was now diluted by Oelsner's record. Nonetheless, Evelyn would be traveling as an athletic ambassador for the United States instead of as the daughter of an Air Force sergeant. Karin Smith was again on the team with her. They competed in dual meets against the Soviets in Kiev and the West Germans in Stuttgart, and then in Italy in invitational meets. U.S. team athletes truly were ambassadors, especially when competing in the Soviet Union. The U.S. State Department sent a representative to talk to the American athletes about their responsibilities, about competing in the spirit of good sportsmanship, and about the rules of international etiquette. Evelyn and Karin would have no problem, but it was scary going into enemy territory where freedom of speech did not exist. (It was rumored that certain athletes on U.S. teams in the 1960s had been used as couriers to deliver secret documents to agents behind the iron curtain, and thoughts of espionage made for more tension than usual.)

By September a tired Evelyn went to the World

Cup meet in Düsseldorf, West Germany, to race against the new world record holder, Marlies Oelsner. Worn out by the long college season and the summer's grueling travel and running, Evelyn didn't have a chance. She placed fifth in the 100 meters and fourth in the 200 meters, and she and Rosalyn Bryant dropped the baton in their relay race. She returned to California humiliated.

Immediately, Tyrone and other coaches confronted her with their usual reason for her poor showing: poor coaching. They again offered themselves as male coaches who knew the science of sprinting better than a housewife (me!).

Evelyn didn't let their remarks fester inside her. She came to me and accepted my answer.

"Your goal this year was to take the double double. You did it, getting the American two-hundred record for dessert. We can't help it if your demanding spring schedule got you ready too early for the World Cup. No other collegians competed at their best in Düsseldorf either. When the World Cup comes again in 1979, I'll have you peaked for revenge."

CHAPTER EIGHT

Dollars Make Sense

"You've been invited to run the sixty-yard dash in the Los Angeles Invitational." (I won't give the sponsor's name for this meet whose promoter had no respect for women's events and to this day discriminates against us.) "How about it?" I asked Evelyn the day after New Year in 1978.

"OK, I guess."

"This will be a chance for you to test your new start that we've been slaving over. With only sixty yards, you won't be able to rely on your finishing gears to win. The start is everything indoors."

We arrived early to give Evelyn time to adjust to the wild sights and sounds inside the arena. "This doesn't seem like a track meet," she said, taking in the circuslike smells of popcorn, hot dogs, and

nachos, mixed with cigarette smoke. The only familiar smell was atomic balm, a strong wintergreen
rubbing compound used by some athletes to warm
up their muscles.

"Watch out for the miles of TV cables scattered
underfoot," I cautioned. "You'll have to jog through
this milling crowd. So stay alert."

There were also obstacles on the steeply banked
wooden track. Runners faced the real possibility
of finding a pole-vaulter's pole falling across their
path or a 16-pound rubber-coated shot bouncing
from lane to lane. With the noisy crowd seated so
close to the track, it was often impossible for the
runners to hear the starter's commands.

"Where are the dancing bears and clowns?" Evelyn asked with a snicker. (Then seeing the shot-
putters walking into the arena, I answered, "I don't
know, but there is the pachyderm parade.")

Before each event the athletes were introduced
by a long-winded announcer, his booming voice
trying to stir up excitement from the noisy spectators. I tried to listen for the first call of Evelyn's
event. "What time is it?" asked Evelyn as beads
of sweat dripped from her forehead.

"Your race is in twenty minutes. You should
go out to the track and practice some starts. Has
Vicki stretched you out yet?"

"Just finished. Here, please pin my number on
my back." She gave me a handful of small safety

pins along with the stiff paper number that was too large for her small torso.

"They sure don't make these numbers with women in mind," I remarked as I folded the edges down, leaving just the number to show.

"Oooo." She wiggled. "How can your hands be so cold?"

"Coaches get nervous too. I'm as scared as you are."

"But you don't have to go out there in front of all those people and take most of your clothes off like I do."

"You don't have to stand helplessly on the sidelines searching for clues about how your athlete will perform," I replied, trying not to stick her with the pin.

"I guess."

Evelyn was too nervous to listen to what I was saying until I faced her and put both my hands on her shoulders. "With all the weight training and practice starts you've done, you're much stronger than you have ever been. Just concentrate in the blocks. You'll be fine."

Evelyn answered me with silence accompanied by a look of "Whatever you say."

"You'll win if you come out of your blocks with the pack."

By the time the runners were on their marks, my heart rate was over 180 and my cold hands felt as if they were below 32 degrees Fahrenheit. With the starter's "Set!" I began silently counting just as Evelyn was supposed to be doing: "One thousand one. One thousand two."

She was gone. Out first!

Then I heard the disappointing "bang" of the recall starter's gun that signified a false start. When the starter stepped into Evelyn's lane, I knew the false start had been charged to her. (Only one false start is allowed each athlete. The second false start disqualifies her from the competition.) I took a deep breath, trying to relax and hoping she would do the same. I could tell by the way she walked back to her blocks that she was furious with herself. She had never false started before. I yelled, "Take it easy!" Amazingly, she heard me. She stood still for a moment, as if her blue spikes were glued to the track. She drew a deep breath, then quickly got into her blocks.

With her next start, the words "Yes, yes, yes, yes, yes" gushed from my mouth in relief I couldn't contain. Evelyn held the lead all the way to the finish line.

Because of their momentum, the sprinters kept moving beyond the finish line into a tunnel under the grandstands. I waited for Evelyn to come jogging back, her arms raised in victory. When I saw the others in her race but not her, I knew what had happened.

Praying she wasn't injured, I began pushing my way through the mob. I knew she'd been so concerned about her start, she hadn't paid much attention to her stop, which was to have been aided by a rope stretched across the track to keep runners from hitting the concrete wall at the end of the straightaway.

Evelyn was in the arms of an official. Before I asked, he said, "She completely flipped over the rope."

"Evelyn, where does it hurt?"

"My knee. My shoulder. I'm okay."

"Take off your spikes and let's go see Vicki," I said, grabbing her sweats.

Always calm in a crisis, Vicki teased, "I see you've invented a new attraction for this circus: rope flipping." After checking her out, Vicki reported, "Nothing broken, nothing strained. You might be a little sore for a few days, but you won't even have to miss one of Connolly's killer practices."

"After my false start I told myself it would never happen again," she told us. Then she smiled at a man of medium height with his hair in cornrows who sauntered toward us.

"Ash, what did you do to yourself?" he asked Evelyn. His shiny leather coat squeaked as he put his arm around her.

"I'd like you to meet my friend Ray Washington," said Evelyn. The two of them jogged off together for her warm-down, leaving me to talk to Vicki. "Mr. Washington might be her first real boyfriend. She once told me she had her first date when she was seventeen. The guy was so rude to her that she's been shy of men. Until now."

Under the grandstand on my way out to the van an Olympic teammate of mine pulled me aside, saying, "Ashford looked great tonight. How much money did you get for this meet?"

"Money? We didn't get any money."

"You let the fastest woman in America run for free? You didn't even get expenses? Dinner? Taxis? Bus fare?" I couldn't tell if he was ridiculing me or surprised at my ignorance.

"Not a dime. Except the meet promoter did give us four free tickets."

"You are so stupid," scoffed my former teammate. "Don't you know that the winners of some of the men's events got a thousand dollars along with the color-TV first prize?" Their coaches probably picked up two hundred, two hundred and fifty each, and at least ten tickets. And that's nothing compared to what some distance runners take home. I'm telling you, it's five thousand bucks every time they step on the track."

I was shocked. "But that's illegal, against both Olympic and collegiate rules."

"All the men are doing it now. They've been ripped off for too long. Haven't you any idea what the meet promoter's making for this show tonight?

Hundreds of thousands of dollars from his sponsor, TV rights, and ticket sales, not to mention program advertising. Why shouldn't the performers get some of it? Movie stars do. Rock singers wouldn't dream of singing for free."

I thought about the plastic juicer Evelyn had won for placing first in her race. It was probably worth ten dollars. Money hadn't crossed her mind. Nor mine. We were grateful simply to compete in a meet that had only six women's events compared to twenty for men.

"Look, if you need help dealing with meet promoters, call me."

"Thanks," I said, wondering if I could ever bring myself to break the rules that prevented Evelyn from legally taking cash. Receiving equipment, uniforms, and shoes free from shoe companies was accepted, however, and when my Olympic teammate, who worked for a shoe company, asked if Evelyn needed any more shoes or training clothes, I replied, "She always needs more shoes. Don't forget her size is five and a half."

Late that night when I got home, Harold helped me think about what I'd been told at the meet. "For years," he said, "male athletes have been paid cash by meet promoters. It's not uncommon for shoe companies to pay athletes to wear their products. Runners used to get hundred-dollar bills stuffed into the toes of shoes they were given to wear at big meets, but now the shoe companies are putting the athletes on their payrolls, making them consultants, so they are not technically breaking the rules."

Now I was feeling exploited. Women were part of the show too, but we were still getting nothing.

Harold went on. "College athletes are virtual slaves, especially the stars who can make far more money than their scholarship is worth. They're held in bondage to their colleges while coaches, athletic directors, and officials have cold hard cash to put in their pockets. With so much pressure to perform for their schools, many student-athletes don't even get their diplomas."

Harold had been fighting for athletes' rights for years, and he knew what he was talking about. "Evelyn would be a fool not to take something when she's so poor that she can't even buy a new pair of jeans without worry."

"I'll think about it."

Not being able to sleep, I got up and went for a walk. It seemed that no matter what success I had, there was always some criticism that kept me from enjoying it. I'd finally been able to help Evelyn perfect a fast start, but no one said "Good job!" about that. Now this money problem. I was confident that I knew what it took to develop a world-class athlete. The criticism from other coaches about my coaching ability hurt, but I could shrug it off, confident that I was pioneering a new path for women that those coaches didn't understand. But

I wasn't savvy enough to handle the money-versus-amateurism issue that was changing my sport into big business.

It was a hard decision to make. I eventually did accept money for Evelyn, who wanted and needed it, but not while she was in school.

CHAPTER NINE

A Baby, a Wedding, and a Big Breakthrough

"Will you still be able to coach when you get bigger?" Dr. Holland asked me when I told her I was pregnant.

"If Chinese women can have babies while working in rice paddies, I can coach my team at Drake. Besides, my baby's not due until summer," I answered. "My main concern is that a new baby will be more than I can handle and still coach a team without domestic help at home for next season. I need a higher salary. As it is, the new men's assistant coach is making more than twice my salary [approximately $18,500 to my now $8,000], and I have more experience and responsibility than he has. Doesn't Title IX assure me of some parity?"

"Don't make trouble for me. I'm giving you as much money as my budget will allow." Dr. Holland took my mention of Title IX as a threat that I might challenge the school under the new equality laws.

Without the raise Harold had to continue working at two jobs, teaching high school English during the day and English as a second language to adults at night school. I would have no help with the children and chores. Because of my low pay he considered my coaching merely a hobby. "You won't be able to care for our new baby and the other children and still coach a university team," he said during a quarrel one day. Sobbing, I yelled back, "Oh, Harold, all you want me to do is stay at home and clean toilets! I've promised Evelyn I'll coach her until the next Olympics."

At that, Adam, two and a half years old now, started to cry. Bradley, age twelve, begged me with his eyes. "Stay home, Mom," he seemed to say.

Later, after we'd placed second in the National Collegiate Championships in Tennessee (Evelyn ran a PR in the 100 of 11.16), I went to Dr. Holland with another plea. "If you can't get me more money, will you at least let me take a year's leave of absence to settle down my family after my baby is born?"

"There is no such thing as a 'leave' for part-time employees. But don't worry. You've done such good work here, we'll always have a job for you."

My assistant, Coach Scod I'll call him, was eager to become head coach. "Your family needs you at home. I'll be glad to take care of your athletes until you come back next year." He turned up one evening at my house in Venice and asked for all my workouts, which I gave to him.

The parting from my team came at a surprise shower the athletes gave me. They were excited about putting their hands on my large stomach and feeling the baby moving from side to side. "She's a jumper," declared six-foot-tall *Glamour* magazine cover girl Cindy Gilbert. "No, she's a half miler and genius like me," piped up Debbie Roberson, a prelaw major whose parents were both doctors. Convinced I'd have the girl I wanted, the team presented me with nothing but pink presents.

My labor started during the night of July 26. Just after midnight on July 27 I had the baby girl they'd predicted.

Evelyn had taken a break from school and track and had driven to Detroit for a visit with Ray's family. She called me from there to hear about my baby. Her voice sounded far away. "What will you name her?" She and the other athletes had made many suggestions during the past spring, but I'd taken Bradley's idea for his sister's name.

"Shannon Elizabeth Corbett Connolly."

"With a name that long she should be a queen. How do you feel?"

It seemed strange, yet good, for Evelyn to be asking me the question I was always asking her. "I feel lighter than I did a few hours ago."

"Ray and I just got married. On Shannon's birthday."

"What?"

"Pat, I got married. You are the first to know. I haven't told my mother yet. My dad will be furious."

"I'm—I'm so surprised. I don't know what to say."

"I'm surprised, too. Ray's mother here in Detroit is a minister. She thought we should get married."

"Congratulations, Mrs. Washington. And when will I see you again?"

"We're going to Florida to visit my parents in their new home and then back to California in August to register for school. I have to go now. 'Bye."

Oh, good grief. I hope she doesn't get pregnant, I thought as I hung up the phone. Maybe her marriage is good, though. Dating can be a distraction from serious training, and single athletes tend to get sick more frequently than do married athletes.

Shannon was only a few weeks old when Evelyn and Ray brought her a mint-green layette and a pair of ribbon-tied shoes. "Ray loves to go shopping." The bride beamed proudly. "Besides, you're usually barefoot, and we were worried that you wouldn't get any shoes for Shannon." The newlyweds were living at her apartment in Westwood near the UCLA campus. That worked out well with

Mr. and Mrs. Washington bring a new outfit to Shannon, here nestled in Evelyn's arm.   G. Lahey

Evelyn's new job at the Nike shoe store, also in Westwood. Nike willingly gave her time off for school, training, and competing. In return she wore their shoes and clothes at races, where she was America's fastest woman, a notable advertisement.

Evelyn now had to decide what to do about school. She still hadn't found an interesting major at UCLA, and she was on the verge of dropping out. "If you're not coaching the team this year, does that mean Scod will be my coach?"

"You're the star. Of course Scod wants you on the team even if you train with me separately. Or you could sit this year out and enroll in courses at a nearby junior college to get your grade-point average up. That way you will still have one season of eligibility left when I return to UCLA next year. That's my choice for you."

"I want you to be my coach. Since you said I must train twice a day in order to beat the East Germans, and I have to work at the Nike store, I think I'll take a break from school until after the Olympics."

"You still need to take a couple of courses so that you can return to UCLA in good standing for your senior year."

"I'll think about it."

Training alone at Drake. Until 1980 pacing Evelyn in her mile time-trials was easy for me. By 1984 she could beat me at every distance up to four miles. Her p.r. of 2:11.0 in the 800m beat my former American record by 2 seconds.
K. S. Photos

I didn't push school on her that year.

For the first time Evelyn and I were training alone together, if you don't count Shannon, who was bundled in her stroller. I took her along to the track with us until an unusually cold and rainy winter set in. Then Harold said, "We'll find a way to pay a baby-sitter a couple of hours a day." He was as convinced as I of Evelyn's talents. He did say, however, that there were two things that I could be doing for Evelyn to insure her success. He brought them up one evening in the kitchen as I made a birthday cake for Bradley. "Money and drugs," he began.

I began whipping the cake batter furiously.

"You are so stubborn," said my husband. "Other coaches are getting cash wherever they can for their athletes. You've been letting Evelyn practically starve because you won't negotiate some appearance dollars for her. She has to stand on her feet all day at the store, and yet you still think she has a chance to beat talented athletes who don't ever work?"

"Under-the-table money deals seem so dirty to me. I'd have to sell Evelyn like a piece of meat." But then I gave in a little. "I'll let her run with a club. That way we can get legal expense money from the meet promoters, because the clubs turn that money over to the athlete. Besides, the club manager can do the negotiating and I'll stick to coaching and planning Evelyn's competitive schedule around her training needs rather than around dollars."

"Good. What are you going to do about steroids? I've heard that everyone who's any good is using them nowadays."

"Everyone is *not* using them! You know how I feel about drugs. They're out of the question. Evelyn's talent and my patience are enough."

"Get this straight. I don't want Evelyn or any woman to use steroids, but you both have to know what you are up against. Evelyn should make the decision for herself. It's her career, not yours. Being an Olympic champion will change her life, might even make her rich. You owe it to Evelyn to tell her objectively about drugs. She's an adult. She can think for herself."

I was getting angrier by the second, scooping the cake batter into pans and slamming them into the oven. "I will *never* be objective about steroids," I screamed.

Harold had won his Olympic gold medal and broken the world record in an era before drugs, when peanut butter and raw eggs were what athletes took to get stronger. But Harold was now concerned that the time had come when a natural athlete like Evelyn didn't have much of a chance to be the best without the help of steroids. He had testified in the U.S. Senate about the dangers of drug use by athletes and he had heard testimony of how widespread drug use was. "I know of women athletes who've taken just five milligrams of Winstrol [an anabolic steroid] a day. They made remarkable improvements right away and suffered no side effects. Evelyn might as well know the facts."

"Go ahead. You can tell her about it. If she wants drugs, I'm finished with her." I threw the dripping cake beaters into the sink.

The next time Evelyn came to our house, I asked her to stay for dinner. After the children left the table Harold began to share what he'd heard from other coaches and athletes who talked openly about how steroids had helped them make big improvements in a short time. I sat at the table nursing Shannon, now and then stealing glances at Evelyn's face. Her puzzlement turned to amazement as Harold ended: "There's a doctor nearby who gives drugs to athletes and monitors their health. They don't have to worry about overdoses or bad drugs or not passing the official drug tests at track meets."

Poor Shannon was getting curdled milk from her upset mother. I waited nervously for Evelyn's answer.

She looked Harold straight in the eyes. "Drugs are not for me," she said with absolute conviction. "I want to find out how good I am. If I take drugs, I'll never know. Besides, it's cheating."

Overwhelmed with her resolve, and thankful that at least someone listened to my team lectures, I said, "I love you, Evelyn. I'll do anything I can to help you be the best."

Together we would find out for ourselves, for all women, for all athletes, and for our children, if talent, hard work, and patience can win out against drugs in the end.

Our resolve to beat the odds kept us focused on the '79 World Cup and, beyond it, the 1980 Olympics. I increased Evelyn's training load so much, I was scared she'd get injured: five days a week, four to six hours a day in double sessions at speeds faster than ever before. We had help from sprinter Elliot Mason, a doctor of psychology who joined our little team and paced Evelyn through her sprint trials and longer runs. Already faster than any woman, Elliot was able to push Evelyn to new personal records. He was someone we could talk to about all aspects of Evelyn's career. His sage advice smoothed rough spots in Evelyn and Ray's marriage. Sometimes it seemed that Elliot was sent from heaven to get us both through our workouts as well as help with tough decisions we had to make.

But Harold had been right about unbelievable improvements by Evelyn's competitors. That May Evelyn was once again beaten to her goal by an East German. This time Marita Koch was the first to run under 22.0 seconds in the 200 meters, destroying the world record with a time of 21.71! "These East Germans are robbing me of all my goals," Evelyn told me at practice. "I'm sick of it.

They can't be training harder than I am." In frustration Evelyn made tight fists and started to scream. Then she darted away and disappeared for an hour before she collected herself and returned ready to fight back. Again I didn't want any excuses to build up in Evelyn's mind, so I said, "Marita Koch is a very talented sprinter. We don't know if she used drugs or not, but it's possible she didn't. If she ran that fast, so can you."

As America's reigning "Queen of Sprints," Evelyn received increasing attention from sports reporters. But unlike many star athletes, she was bothered by their uninvited phone calls and visits to the track. Shy and reticent under any conditions, she had been sadly embarrassed by her own halting answers to questions at a track writers' luncheon in the past. My mistake! I took her to it, then afterward promised, "I'll never put you through that again. Let's make a pact. No more interviews until you've practiced your public speaking. Your running will do the talking." From then on I acted as a buffer. Reporters had to see me first and were rarely allowed to interview Evelyn.

To improve her confidence we played interview games. I asked typical questions and helped her form answers.

"When the TV interviewer walks up to you right after a race, Evelyn, and shoves a microphone into your face and says, 'Nice race. How do you feel?'

you have several options for an answer, but don't just say 'Fine.' "

Catching on, Evelyn answered, "I felt strong coming out of the blocks. I was never aware of the other runners."

"All right. You can answer a general question with whatever's on your mind, but don't give one-word responses, because it makes you look lazy or ignorant." Holding a shoe like a TV mike in Evelyn's face I said, "Are you surprised your coach is giving you time off to go to Jamaica for a fun, pressureless meet?"

"I am most pleasantly surprised."

I didn't go with Evelyn to Jamaica that May. Her training had been so time-consuming and intense that she deserved some fun alone with Ray. (Her invitation to the meet included all expenses for two, not three.) She phoned me from Kingston right after her race with the news that she'd broken the American record, held by Wyomia Tyus. "Eleven-o-six, can you believe it?" Evelyn shouted over the phone's static.

"Yes, I believe it. I'll have to send you to romantic tropical islands more often," I shouted back. The next morning I rushed out to get the paper with the results of her new record. In my excitement I must have read the article at least a dozen times.

It had been more than ten years since an American

had held the title of fastest woman in the world. American women had all but given up competing internationally, as I had, because of the dominance of Russians, East Germans, and other Europeans who had financial support and who we thought used steroids. Now in the summer of 1979 there seemed to be a chance for America to reclaim the sprint title. Brenda Morehead and Chandra Cheeseborough were in the best condition of their lives and determined to make the U.S. World Cup team. According to their coach they'd had enough of losing to Evelyn.

But in June, at the U.S. Championships at Mount SAC (Mt. San Antonio College), their newfound speed merely pushed Evelyn to run another American record for the 100 meters: 10.97!

She did it! She went under eleven seconds. This was the second-fastest performance ever. She also won the 200 meters with a promising wind-aided time of 22.20, shutting out the other Americans from the only World Cup spot in both sprints.

Marlies Gohr (unlike Evelyn, Marlies Oelsner took on her husband's surname) and Marita Koch would be at the World Cup games to defend their world records.

I met Evelyn in Europe, where she won every invitational meet she entered. European meet promoters were clamoring for more Ashford, but I played the spoiler once again by insisting she run no more meets—for any amount of money—and

The coach, Evelyn, and Elliot after her first sub 11:00 second
100m at Mt. SAC National Championships.   K. S. Photos

that she go early to Montreal, Canada, and get ready for the World Cup.

Evelyn's first World Cup appearance had been disastrous. She had to redeem herself here in Montreal. I slept on the floor, giving the only bed to Ray and Evelyn. Our club manager said we couldn't afford two separate rooms from the money Evelyn had earned in Europe. Our crowded room led Ray to question other American athletes about their expense money, and eventually he discovered that Evelyn was not getting all the money she should have. When Ray explained all this to us, Evelyn asked me to act as her business manager from then on. I agreed, reluctantly. "I'd better do it since there's no one else we can trust. But stealing's the least of your worries. You're about to race against the world, and you sound like you're coming down with a cold."

"My throat does hurt a little."

"I'll call Doc Brown and ask what medications you can take. Coricidin works for me, but it might be a banned substance."

Hundreds of drugs, including many that seemed to be nothing more than harmless remedies, were on the list of banned substances. Some of these contained stimulants and were believed to help runners run faster, jumpers jump higher, and so forth.

Doc Harmon Brown, the United States team doctor, warned me against Coricidin D, the white tablets. These were banned. Yet Coricidin red tablets would be okay for Evelyn's cold. I was irritated by having to watch every little thing that went into her mouth. "It's ludicrous. For you to catch the cheaters we all have to suffer. And by the way, from what I've heard, the drug tests don't stop anyone. Cheaters know how to beat the tests."

Ray, always aware of the media, was concerned about Evelyn's appearance. "Your braids are getting nappy, Ash. Why don't you take them out," he begged her. Evelyn glanced in the mirror, agreed with him, and then promptly forgot all about it. She had racing on her mind.

Only the official team coaches were allowed to be on the warm-up field outside the stadium with their athletes. That was a hard-and-fast rule. But the head U.S. coach looked the other way when I snuck onto the field with Evelyn to help her go through her stretching routine. I chose my last words carefully, remembering how they always affected Evelyn. "You won't be running with the worries and doubts that drug cheaters carry on their shoulders. You have a clear conscience. You've worked hard to find out just how good you are. It's going to be fun to watch you. You've already won as far as I am concerned."

Evelyn had already begun disappearing into herself. She said nothing. Her total concentration was a good sign. I needed to see that, because her last tune-up time trials had been atrocious. Evelyn, without realizing what she was doing, had started to save her energy for the big showdown to come.

There were no heats. No semifinals to relieve the jitters. All competitions were finals. Evelyn had drawn lane two on the track. Marita Koch, considered by experts to be the greatest woman sprinter of all time, would be in an outside lane, where she had the advantage of not having to run as sharp a turn as Evelyn.

The runners got into their blocks. But then, just as the starter was about to say, "Set," Evelyn stood up and raised her hand.

"What's she doing?" Ray asked me.

"Must be something wrong with her blocks and she's had the composure not to panic," I replied, trying not to show that I was shaking. *BANG!* "Ray, that's the start of her life. Look. She's already made up the stagger."

"She's got it, she's got it." Ray took over the yelling. Now we both felt certain that no one, not even the powerfully surging Koch, would catch our little sprinter down the straightaway. As Evelyn crossed the finish line, she glanced at the stadium clock: 21.83, an American record. Koch had 22.02.

I didn't go to the press room for Evelyn's first interview since our pact. I learned later that she'd been as tense there as I'd been in the grandstand

The big breakthrough, beating Koch in the 200m dash at the World Cup in 1979. Glancing at the clock on the scoreboard, Evelyn was more concerned about her time than her hair.

at the race's start. Jon Hendershott of *Track and Field News* magazine reported that "Ashford was uncomfortable dealing with her own thoughts or having to express them in public. And when she tried to leave the podium, reporters converged on her like steel to a magnet. Everyone wanted to know more about this young star who could run so fast—away from her competition and from the press."

The morning papers were filled with pictures of "The Amazing Ashford." Ray read us the articles at breakfast, and his glee was infectious. Evelyn loved the reports of "stunned East Germans." I said I hoped Marlies Gohr would still be stunned during the 100-meter race that afternoon. "Let her think about Ashford for a change!"

There were no problems at the starting line of the 100. Evelyn assumed control of the race at 60 meters, finishing first in a time of 11.06 to Gohr's 11.17. Back in the pressroom after her defeat of Gohr and the others in 100 meters, Evelyn's confidence made her interviews easier. "My start wasn't as good as in the two hundred, but I knew I was going to win from the beginning. I just knew it."

"What were you feeling?" asked Kenny Moore of *Sports Illustrated*.

"Relief. But the next instant I was afraid. There was a vacuum in front of me. 'What do I do now?' I thought. There wasn't the ecstatic reaction I expected to have. I'd done everything I wanted to

Beating her second world record holder (Gohr) in two days, Evelyn became the premier sprinter in the world. The expressions on their faces show who will win. Tony Duffy/Allsport

do, and it was like I was saying to myself, 'Is that all there is?' "

I wasn't at that interview, or else I would have pointed out that there was much more for Evelyn to do. The coach sees no vacuum.

CHAPTER TEN

Shattered Dreams

Evelyn was now a cover girl, one of the few women runners of the 1970s to be chosen by *Track and Field News* for the honor. Feature articles in *Sports Illustrated* and *Jet* magazine gave a further boost to her earning power and helped us arrange a more generous shoe contract, this time with a shoe company I'll call RIO. The company paid her $800 and me $200 per month, not much by some measures, but at least she didn't have to work in a shoe store as she had for Nike. Ray especially enjoyed wearing the latest-style sports clothes that came with the RIO contract. He had a flare for fashion.

"He's always so perfectly dressed," Evelyn said. Evelyn preferred wearing her old comfortable tights and T-shirts at workouts. "I'm just a slob."

Not only was there no "vacuum," but we were right smack in the middle of track-and-field's promotion show. There were more expectations and demands on Evelyn than ever before. Her World Cup victories had given us the encouragement we needed to plow ahead with our rigorous training schedule, but now we were in a fishbowl, and all privacy was gone.

Tired of living like paupers, the Washingtons rented a one-bedroom apartment in Hollywood and traded in their old broken-down Dodge for a used but more reliable Audi.

Ray had come from a family of thirteen children, and by those standards Evelyn and Ray were already famous and rich. Along with Evelyn's sisters and Ray's family there now always seemed to be someone staying with them. Evelyn would bring one problem after another to our workouts. I tried to talk to her, to calm her down and get her mind back on the track. Again and again I reminded her that we had to hold things together until next summer's Olympic Games. "Evelyn, with the pressure of your career, these new family problems can be draining. In less than one year you will be an Olympic champion with three gold medals. Then you'll have more time for family. You can't carry them on your shoulders now."

Usually she shrugged off my advice about the many people around her. She couldn't say no to the family's demands that were ruining her concentration. From my conversations with her and one of her sisters I understood that people were saying things like "Pat Connolly doesn't love you the way we do. Pat's not blood, and blood is thicker than water. We'll always love you. When you can't run anymore, Pat will be gone." Whether those were the exact words or not, it was clear that some of her relatives were jealous of my relationship and influence with her. To them I was standing in the way of her earning power when I didn't let Evelyn run in every meet to which she was invited.

This was my fourth year of coaching Evelyn. We'd become so close that I considered her one of my best friends and believed I was one of hers. Like most friends we would shop for shoes and clothes together, go on eating binges (we once consumed a pound of See's chocolates in one afternoon!), discuss books and movies, and talk about current events and politics. We also shared our personal problems. Evelyn always had a patient ear for me to vent my family frustrations. (It wasn't easy being a stepmother.) She'd offer sympathy and statements like "Your life is more entangled than the soaps. No wonder you don't like to watch them."

I proudly wore the gold chain and winged-foot medallion Evelyn and Ray had given me. I took our pastimes for granted until the day Evelyn accused me of intolerance. "You really don't understand what it's like to be black, do you Pat?"

"What do you mean?" I kept my voice steady, but I was floored.

"Well, you think Ray should have a job, but it's a lot harder for young black men to get the jobs they want than it is for young white men."

"What you say is true and I do understand. Just like all women, black men have to be twice as good as white men to have a chance. But that doesn't mean they shouldn't try to get the job they want."

"Ray wants to play basketball for a living. He's trying out for the Globetrotters."

"I know he loves the sport. He's been so encouraging to Bradley's basketball game." (The tough pick-up games Ray took Brad to around town had really helped my son.)

My children often came with me to practice. Here Bradley tries some donkey kicks while I stretch out Evelyn. (PNF)
K. S. Photos

"Has Ray thought about getting his degree and a teaching credential so he can coach?"

"Don't you know? Blacks aren't given the good coaching jobs," Evelyn said in a sullen voice I scarcely recognized. "And remember when you said you wanted to coach a white sprinter? I guess I'm not good enough for you either."

"Good Lord, Evelyn. Being a coach is like being a parent with many children, each unique and well loved. I'd like to coach a white sprinter just to break the black-only stereotype. I've told you I myself could have been a sprinter but I wasn't given the chance because I was white. Americans, including most coaches, believe that only blacks can sprint and only whites can pole-vault. I'd like to coach a black pole-vaulter just because there aren't any brothers who've been top vaulters."

After all the years she'd seen me in action, she must have known that color didn't influence my judgment of people. Sure we'd joked about unusual black names, noting that they were like Mormon names: Shellsea, Lamar, Thelma, Chalisa, LaVonna, Germaine. But she'd known about and met some of my dear black friends, some of whom had been national and Olympic teammates of mine. I don't think of my friends in colors. The color of their skin is not a description of each one's unique personality and character. They are just my friends.) Back in the days when I'd been competing, I'd refused to eat in restaurants where my black teammates weren't served. In protest I'd used "Negro" drinking fountains and "colored" bathrooms, furious at people who'd thought up such things. I'd been active in Dr. Martin Luther King, Jr.'s movement for racial equality. I signed initiatives, and had even left my church when I realized that church policy kept blacks out. I took a stand when I was kicked out of my apartment for entertaining "coloreds" on the premises.

But there in the fall of 1979 I was suddenly Evelyn's *white* coach, a racist resented by some for having too much control over her.

I grew careful about every word I spoke at our workouts for fear of being thought a bigot. I agonized with Evelyn about social injustices whenever they came up as a topic of conversation. I agreed that she would earn more money if she were America's fastest woman *and* white. "Of course I know that the white people who control the advertising dollars on Madison Avenue prefer white performers to endorse their products." Pausing and looking her straight in the eye, I added, "Don't get mad at me because I'm white. I love you as you are. I wouldn't change anything about you."

Times were changing and taking Evelyn along for the ride. Black pride was good, but it also had a negative side in which all whites—not just the bigots—were stigmatized. I had enjoyed many intimate interracial relationships, but now black-white friendships were getting harder to make and maintain.

Whether or not she believed me about the color of our friendship, she trusted my coaching. We continued training. Sometimes we even laughed our way through the hard parts. After my old van stalled on the San Diego Freeway for the zillionth time and we had to push it to an exit, I joked, "I'll bet the East Germans haven't thought of this training method."

"Pat, only *you* would consider pushing a one-ton van down a freeway wearing high heels and a skirt *training*." Dripping with sweat, Evelyn broke down and howled with me.

Karin, who had also left school to train with a javelin specialist, showed up one day with news of the latest rumor. "Pat, some of the male coaches have put out the word that you are gay."

"Karin, that lie is typical of the way men try to discredit strong, successful women. I am used to it. Though it's not true, there is nothing we can do about it. I love Evelyn and you very much — like my own sisters, but not sexually. If other people are jealous of us, that's their problem."

Most mornings we used Drake Stadium's track even though I had not returned to coaching the UCLA women's track team that fall. I had been squeezed out of the job by Coach Scod. My former assistant had arranged himself a two-year contract with Dr. Holland shortly after I'd left UCLA with her promise to take me back "anytime."

We had just settled into a demanding training program when President Jimmy Carter threatened to boycott the Olympics in Moscow. He announced he'd keep our Olympic team home in the U.S. unless the Soviets pulled out of Afghanistan, a country they had recently invaded. I told Evelyn the news while we were at practice.

"That's not funny, Pat."

"I'm not trying to be funny. I heard it on my car radio on the way here."

"It won't happen. I'm going to the Olympics next summer and that's that," Evelyn insisted.

I was so worried about the boycott hurting Evelyn that I phoned my friend Bob Caughlan, who worked for President Carter in Washington, D.C. "Can Carter mean what he said?" I asked straight out.

"Carter does mean it. He may be sorry he said it without much thought, but now that the word's out, he's going to stick to it."

"Damn, damn, damn! Doesn't he realize it won't work? Military strategists don't give a hoot about sports." Bob, always gentle and tolerant, knew better than to argue with me.

Evelyn simply refused to believe in the boycott. "There must be other things the United States of America can do to force the hand of the Russians besides keeping amateur athletes home from the Olympic Games."

She was a superstar on the indoor circuit that winter of 1980, often making as much as $1,000 per meet. I formed my own club, The Medalist Track Club, so I could legally accept money from meet promoters for her. My coaching fee was ten percent of what she made on the track. I accompanied Evelyn to the meets to deal with promoters and to anticipate any problems at the track that might cause injuries. Evelyn had competed without me in many meets over the years, mostly because we didn't have the money or child care for me to go with her. Since many of those meets were not covered by radio or TV, she'd either phone me with her results or I would search for them in the paper the next day. Now promoters paid my way.

Nineteen eighty! The Olympic year. Our four-year plan was on schedule. In Toronto, Canada, we relaxed before the indoor race by shopping in what was then the world's largest mall. I talked Evelyn into buying a pair of flashy blue disco tights to keep her legs warm during her race in the cold stadium. (Indoor tracks are sometimes laid down directly on ice-hockey rinks.) That night she introduced disco tights to the track world, where, for a change, she drew admiring stares for her clothes. She won her race easily. So far, so good. But back at the hotel we heard again that President Carter could not be talked out of his boycott.

"Evelyn, sooner or later you must accept the reality that you are not going to the Olympics this year."

"I won't, I won't, I won't. Please don't lose faith, Pat. Something will happen. I'll get to go. I know I will." Evelyn looked sadder than sad, sitting up in bed, crying, trying to read two romance novels at a time, trying to eat but losing her appetite and pushing her favorite chicken and fettuccine around on the plate. "They can't do this. They just can't do this," she said over and over, throwing her books at the window and herself onto the bed, where she pounded her pillow and continued to cry.

Just then we heard a knock at the door. It was Debbie Roberson, now a law student at Howard University but still competing. She had run in the 800 meters that night. Seeing Evelyn distraught and me fit to be tied, Debbie invited us both to join a group of athletes at a party. "You old married ladies are too serious all the time. Come have some fun," she urged.

We got dressed and went out, only to find our party was little more than a group of Olympic hopefuls sitting around in a disco discussing Jimmy Carter. I suggested we all boycott the boycott, that we travel to Moscow as individuals and compete without Carter's blessing.

"We'll never be allowed back into the U.S." claimed someone at our table.

With that Evelyn decided to order a drink of

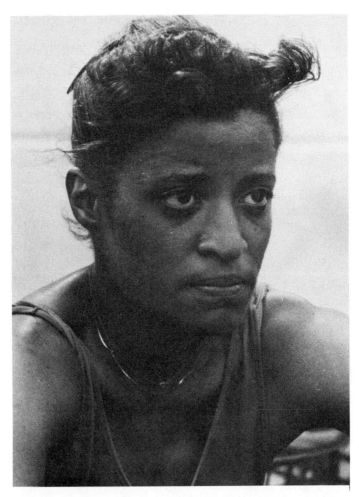

Debbie Roberson, the first athlete I ever coached, was disap-pointed about the boycott too.   Jeff Johnson

hard liquor, something she'd never tried before. "What's a screwdriver?" she asked after scanning the list of drinks on the menu.

"It's orange juice and vodka," we all told her.

"Fine. I'll have vodka. Isn't that what Russians drink?"

It didn't take much alcohol for Evelyn to get

quite silly and, for a moment, to forget the boycott. I felt like getting plastered myself but stayed sober to take care of her. Soon she couldn't stand on her own two legs. She laughed and laughed and laughed, weaving among the tables. I had to grab her before she fell to the floor.

By the time I got her back to our room, Evelyn was crying, "I'm so dizzy. The room is spinning."

"Evelyn, if you throw up, you will start to feel better. The alcohol has poisoned you." As I watched her retching, I thought, *So much for diversion. She's still going to have to face the boycott, but now she'll have a big headache to go along with it.*

At our next workout back home Evelyn was all optimism once again. She said, "Elliot and I have prayed about the Olympics. You must have faith that our prayers will be answered."

"Faith without works is dead," I quoted from the New Testament. "You and the other top athletes will have to lead the opposition to the boycott. I've called Edwin Moses, Mary Decker, Arnie Robinson, Kate Schmidt, and some coaches. They want to go to Moscow as much as we do, and they're eager to make Carter change his mind. He will have to listen to our side if we take it to the press. Evelyn, you'll have to speak out with them."

"Me? You know how I hate interviews."

"We'll rehearse what you should say. I'm setting up a press conference in Palo Alto to coincide with the track meet there at Stanford. The networks,

A press conference planning session in the Connolly dining room. (L to R) Geni (Mary Anne's niece), Adam (with a hunger for knowledge), Harold, Pat, Evelyn, Ray, Mary Anne   G. Lahey

newspapers, Edwin, Mary, and Arnie will all be there."

Evelyn's training suffered as we focused on the boycott. We spent hours sitting on the grass at Drake Stadium, talking politics, pulling the grass, talking bigotry, throwing the grass, and cursing Carter, before we got down to the business of running. Absorbed in our problems, we paid little attention to three men in drab business suits who were in the grandstands taking notes on some days or hiding in the oleanders taking pictures of us on other days. At the end of that week I mentioned it. "That guy on the left looks familiar, but I don't know why."

"Maybe they're East Germans over here to spy on Evelyn. They think they can figure out her training secrets," said Michele Hopper, a middle-distance runner whom I'd begun coaching that year.

Michele Hopper, Evelyn's training partner, wins a race at Drake. For four years they warmed up together, laughed and cried together, and complained about "Killer Connolly" to each other. Bill Leung

Michele was right. The men introduced themselves. The one who spoke the best English invited us to come to Mexico City, where the East German team had been training. They wanted a "friendly" competition between Evelyn and Gohr, Evelyn and Koch. I refused, preferring to meet those archrivals on the track in Moscow.

The East Germans muttered, "Ve hope you vill be zere."

So did we. The press conference, meetings, and lunches in Palo Alto were easier than usual for Evelyn. No one could complain about her inaccessibility. She looked like a young woman lawyer, perfect for the occasion in a suit Ray had helped her choose. My dear friend Mary Anne Sayler, who lived nearby, drove us to the San Francisco airport saying, "Evelyn's become so sophisticated." Mary Anne and her husband, Chuck, had been watching Evelyn at track meets and hosting us in their home since 1976.

The list of people supporting our opposition to the boycott grew longer. Among them were triple jumper Willie Banks and Olympic rower Anita de Franz. They both helped us keep up the pressure on members of Congress. But President Carter's resolve could not be shaken. His people persuaded Olympic sponsors like Levi Strauss to withdraw their financial support, and when the U.S. Olympic Committee, which opposed the idea of a boycott, found its money disappearing, it voted to go along with the President. My own group, of course, had no money to continue the fight. I'd been paying for long-distance phone calls and trips from my own pocket.

Then out of the blue I received a phone call from a woman offering us expense money as well as her office for our headquarters. She said she'd already printed stationery for us to use. The design on the letterhead was Misha Bear, the mascot of Moscow.

The offer tempted me, but the letterhead seemed too Russian even for our group bent on getting to Moscow. I made some phone calls and found out that the woman represented the Communist Party and was trying to manipulate our group to embarrass the U.S. government.

That did it! We were angry at President Carter but not enough to seek Communist help. Evelyn and I—and, I'm sure, many other athletes on different occasions that March—managed to throw world-class tantrums. Kicking, screaming, and pounding the floor until fists hurt didn't change anything, but athletes need physical outlets. Before we resigned ourselves to watching the Olympic Games on TV, I vowed to work to see that Carter did not get reelected that fall.

"There's no reason to train anymore," Evelyn announced, completely despondent one overcast April morning.

"Oh yes there is. The Japanese Federation has

invited us to a series of three meets in Japan. They'll pay you $5,000 and all our expenses. They even said I could bring Shannon along since it is such a long trip."

"I'd like to see Japan," she said with little enthusiasm, "but I was prepared for a twelve-course meal, and all they're giving me is this trip—an appetizer." The Olympic disappointment was now permanently in her voice.

In Hiroshima, Japan, we saw real ruins and then films of the devastation done by the atomic bomb.

Photographers followed us everywhere. It wasn't easy schlepping blocks and baby paraphernalia all over Japan in 1980.

We felt less sorry for ourselves, but still Evelyn's love of running didn't return. In each of her races she merely went through the motions. She seemed indifferent to the pain from a strain she developed behind her left knee, even after I warned her to be careful.

"What am I saving myself for?"

When we returned from Japan, I noticed that the maple tree Evelyn had given me in 1976 was leafless and dry. In the past four years it had grown nearly three feet. As I yanked it out of the ground and threw it into the trash, I realized that our "Olympic Tree" had died with our Olympic hopes.

Evelyn's leg was still sore, but she wanted the money she could make in the Pepsi Meet held at Drake Stadium on Mother's Day. I let her run, saying, "You have nothing to lose."

She came out of the blocks beautifully in the Pepsi 100 and held the lead for 50 meters before she shot up straight into the air. She'd finally pulled her hamstring muscle as a result of the sore leg she'd neglected in Japan. Standing across the field, I saw Vicki Vodon run onto the track to care for Evelyn, who was by then lying facedown surrounded by various track officials, reporters, and cameramen. Then I saw a man who didn't belong there at all. I broke all speed records running across the infield and narrowly missed being speared by a javelin. Our former club manager, who'd made sleazy sexual overtures to us, already sat at her side pretending to be responsible for her.

I lost my temper, grabbed him, and with all my strength threw him down the track. "He has nothing to do with her! He's just trying to get in front of the cameras," I told the surprised officials. Vicki carried Evelyn to the trainers' tent. There the meet doctor took out a long needle to give Evelyn a shot of cortisone. In five years some doctors still hadn't learned not to inject pulled muscles.

"Please don't do it," I said. "Vicki will ice her leg and wrap it in an ace bandage. That's enough for now."

"But the cortisone will reduce the inflammation and help it heal faster. Evelyn won't be ready to run in the Olympic trials without a shot," the doctor insisted.

"There are *no* Olympics for U.S. athletes. So what's the point of going to the Trials?"

As we left the tent, I heard the doctor say, "That Connolly woman is crazy."

I spun around and retorted, "Someone must have the athletes' best interests at heart."

Our Olympic dream was over. It seemed to me that Evelyn would never train hard again. I felt almost as bad as my broken-hearted sprinter.

Then something happened that made me feel worse than Evelyn, but I didn't dare share it with her at the time. The top Canadian sprint coach came up to me at the track one day with a proposition: "If you and I work together, we can beat the East Germans at their own game. I've been to East Germany, and I know what drugs they're taking and how they monitor them so their athletes can pass the drug tests. I'll share this information with you if you'll tell me what drugs you are giving Evelyn."

When he saw I was speechless, he continued, "Come on. Several American coaches and athletes claim Evelyn's using drugs. Everybody at the top is using them."

"Go to hell. Maybe your athletes need drugs, but Evelyn is so talented and has such a good coach that we don't have to stoop that low."

I raged away from him but hadn't gotten far when it hit me that there was no way I could prove our innocence. The cheaters were justifying their own weaknesses by making everyone look bad. I jumped in my car, drove to the beach, and in T-shirt and shorts jumped into the surf and swam out as fast and as far as I could. It took me a long time to get back to shore, but not as long as it took me to decide to keep coaching.

CHAPTER ELEVEN

The Speed Suit

Harold and I watched the 1980 Olympics in our living room in Venice, California, over 6,000 miles from Moscow.

"If I'd made the team, I would have bought my own ticket to Moscow," I said at the start of the women's pentathlon. "The Russians would be happy to let an American compete."

"Certainly they would, but here at home you'd be viewed as a traitor. You'd be an outcast from the track world for the rest of your life. No one would sponsor your club. You'd be lucky if you ever got another pair of free shoes. Let's forget your 'would haves' and 'could haves.'" Harold had been putting up with my boycott talk for nine long months.

After her injury in May at the Pepsi Meet Evelyn

gave up training. She took off with Ray for a drive to visit his parents in Detroit and later to visit hers in Florida. She didn't phone me again until October. Then she said, "I hate myself. I'm so fat. My body's telling me to run even if my mind isn't."

"Go out and start jogging," I suggested. "You have time to get in shape for the indoor season."

"Good. I need to make some money. I'll give you ten percent if you'll coach me again."

"Money isn't enough to motivate me," I said. "I've watched too many athletes burn themselves out before reaching their full potential. Do you still want to break the world record?"

"Pat, the boycott tore out my soul. I put all my eggs in one basket emotionally and physically, and that's why it took so long for me to accept that I wouldn't have a chance to achieve what I'd been aiming at for four years. I can't do that again."

"But Evelyn, you don't have to wait for the Olympics to break the world record. At every track meet there's a chance for a record."

"I guess. Do you still think I can do it?"

"For the thousandth time, yes. You were running faster in parts of your race than most men. All you need to do is put your best start, best middle, and best finish into one race. You are in your prime, your leg will heal, but you have to want it. Now you'll have time to fully develop your talent instead of retiring as you would have after the Moscow Olympics to a life of banquets and speeches."

"When's practice?"

Here I go again, I said to myself. Back to the agonizing details of planning training schedules. Back to analyzing films until my eyes blurred. Back to giving rubdowns and ice massages. Back to schlepping blocks, measuring tapes, distance-marking cones, spikes, wrenches, starting pistol, shells, and first-aid stuff around the world. And the worst part—dealing with meet promoters, negotiating shoe contracts, and handling all the public and media demands that are made on star athletes. A star is more time-consuming to coach than an entire UCLA team. *Why am I doing this?* I asked myself.

The reasons were the same as before. Like my friend who worked for NASA on projects that might discover life on other planets, I was challenged. I wanted to see some real female speed on planet Earth. Though Evelyn couldn't say it now, I knew she still wanted Olympic gold. She'd once told me, "I want to be the best sprinter of all time—not just my time but all time."

We went to the beach twice a week to train, rain or shine—to Venice Beach, famous for crazy people who strut their stuff on the cement sidewalk bordering the sand. Strolling musicians. Mimes. Bikini-clad roller skaters. Kite flyers. Body builders. A honky-tonk piano player. A grandma on a skateboard with sails to propel her through the parking lot. A crowd of wide-eyed tourists, usually identifiable by their polo shirts and bermuda shorts, watching a tall barefoot woman dressed in old sweats pacing back and forth in the sand yelling to sprinting athletes. Drake Stadium was the hangout for stars; Venice was the habitat for Hollywood rejects. We went there because Venice Beach was convenient to my house and we needed the soft sand to help stretch out the scar tissue from Evelyn's injury as well as strengthen her feet, ankles, and legs. Michele was always with us, and sometimes Elliot, Karin, Debbie, Modupe, Jimmy (my stepson, who was training for the decathlon), Bradley, Adam, or Shannon joined our beach "backbreaker workouts."

Evelyn was no longer afraid to run in the water. We had learned to read each other's moods, to communicate without talking. Much as I tried to keep details of our workouts a surprise, she often guessed my plans just by looking at me. It became a game for me to come up with the unexpected. This kept us both from boredom in a sport that demanded thousands of repetitions.

Three days a week we trained at Drake Stadium, where one glaringly smoggy day Evelyn felt dizzy after her time trials. I cut the practice short but not soon enough, for as we walked to our cars parked on the other side of the campus, she gave a low moan and collapsed. I barely managed to catch her before she hit the ground. On the way down, the spikes from the shoes she carried raked my arm and leg.

No one was around to help. I picked Evelyn up

and started carrying her to my van. "My head," she moaned. "My eyes. It's so bright."

I drove her straight to Dr. Krakovitz, a specialist in holistic medicine. Dr. K opposed using drugs of any kind. He'd volunteered to monitor the health of my athletes because as a doctor he rarely had the chance to work with healthy people. He already knew Evelyn from tests he'd given her two years ago. "She's the healthiest person I've ever tested," he had said then.

"It's too bright in here," Evelyn screamed in his office. She tried to crawl under his desk, out of the light.

"Have you ever had a migraine?" Dr. K asked her.

"A long time ago, in high school."

"Does this feel the same?"

"I guess. Don't talk so loud."

The doctor's voice had been barely above a whisper. "She has a migraine," he whispered now. "Go buy her a bottle of club soda. She can stay under my desk until you come back."

The club soda and an extra two days of rest revived Evelyn, and training went on as scheduled. In time we learned to recognize the symptoms of migraines and to treat them with soda, ice, and massage before they developed into full-blown headaches.

Evelyn's interest in sewing and textiles gave us an interest in common that really paid off. Back in 1980, in Japan, we had met a representative from the company that had made Eric Heiden's speed-skating suit, the one he'd worn to win five Olympic gold medals in the 1980 Winter Games at Lake Placid, New York. I'd asked if such a suit could be made for Evelyn to wear in her races.

"This is not the traditional uniform for track athletes," they replied.

"Not now, but this suit, and variations we'd like you to make for us, will be the traditional clothing of track athletes in years to come. Everyone will want to copy Evelyn. Even men."

The Japanese agreed to humor this unusual woman and her star athlete.

They took Evelyn's measurements. She stood on a chair saying, "If this is what models have to go through, I'm glad I'm not a model." She chose black, beige, purple, and red for her first suits and enthusiastically gave details for each suit's design.

Four bodysuits were made for her (and two for me), yet when it came time to wear one in a meet, Evelyn felt terribly nervous. I wouldn't let her change her mind. "You've got to have style," I exclaimed. "You've got to be more than just another fast runner. This suit will give you media attention, the kind that will help you earn more money. The tight fit of your suit will reduce wind resistance. Less wind, more speed. Also your bra straps and underpants won't show."

As she wiggled into the long-sleeved and hooded

black suit through the neck opening she asked, "How am I supposed to go to the bathroom in this?"

"You don't pee in the suit. You pull the whole thing down first."

"Thanks a lot." Tucking her hair into the hood, she said, "Do I look like the spider lady?"

"No, you look 'faster than a speeding bullet, more powerful than a locomotive,' and very sexy. I think Ray will approve." The suit streamlined her body, making her look taller and accentuating her muscle definition—especially in the rear, where her powerful muscles stood out.

She smiled in the mirror at herself, enjoying my words at the same time. Then, as her expression grew more serious, it seemed that she was wondering, *Is that really me in the slinky black suit?* She had made an amazing transformation over the past five years—from the shy teenager of 1976 into a racing daredevil, unafraid of anyone, competitor or reporter, that January of 1981.

Evelyn was the first to introduce the bodysuit to the track world, but that night in her race, her concentration suffered and she got out of the blocks in second place. She won anyway. Not wanting to be humiliated in her new suit, she ran faster than ever before. *Sports Illustrated* gave the suit more space than her speed, and in days to follow

The speed suit suits speed.   Tony Duffy/Allsport

she was swamped with requests for appearances. I helped her weigh the offers, basing the acceptances on Evelyn's training schedule. I took the blame for saying no to meet promoters and others. In that way I became the buffer—the crazy coach who turned down many "important" people begging for Evelyn's time.

The beige suit was short and sleeveless with a scoop neck, and Evelyn decided to save it for the Outdoor National Championships that were to be held in hot, dry Sacramento in June of 1981. Temperatures there soared above one hundred degrees, leaving the synthetic track soft and mushy, not good conditions for world-record performances that required a hard, bouncy track. At least the heat would keep the sprinters' legs loose and fast. I drove the famous blue van north through the "salad bowl," central California's fertile valleys. Karin Smith was with me, now a member of my Medalist Track Club. Evelyn had flown to Sacramento in order to have more time at home. She was riding back with us, however, and I made it clear she had to take a turn at the wheel. "Drive, not push," I promised. "Not even I, Coach Dracula, would make you push a one-ton van after a race."

The competition at Nationals would be fiercer than ever, for Evelyn had made sprinting glamorous. Improving rapidly was a handful of talented newcomers from Wilt's Wonder Women Track Club.

"What woodwork did they crawl out of?" Evelyn

asked about Wilt's high-stepping sprinters. Evelyn was surprised to see them beat the Tennessee State duo of Morehead and Cheeseborough in the preliminaries.

"They are running well, but not in a class with you," I assured her. "It's good other Americans are coming along. We'll have a relay team to beat East Germany. Great as you are, you can't run relays without teammates."

"I don't care about relays." That response brought a stern lecture from me about how the truly great sprinters in history are more fondly remembered for their come-from-behind relay runs than anything else. But I cut it short as I watched the deep folds of worry form in Evelyn's normally smooth forehead. She looked like the word "uptight" had been invented for her.

The phone kept ringing in our motel rooms, where we'd gone to rest in air-conditioning before the 100-meter final. Local newspapers couldn't wait until after the race to interview Evelyn, the star from nearby Roseville High School. Gary Ginzlinger, the high school coach who had first put her on his boys' team, came to introduce himself to me. We tried to answer questions from reporters, friends, and old coaches graciously, until at last it was time for me to give Evelyn a rubdown and stretch. We always did the stretching to test her muscle balance, but the rubdowns were saved for those times when she felt tight. Her tightness now was more in her mind than in her muscles.

"Evelyn, first you're worried about competitors who aren't in a class with you, then you're exasperated by the demands of celebrity that you sought and got. What's really bothering you?" As I kneaded her legs, I thought, *something is wrong at home.*

"I have to win and make the World Cup team, Pat. I need money again."

"You won't run well with that kind of self-imposed pressure. You mustn't think of anything except what you're supposed to do when the gun goes off. Concentrate on your start. The rest will take care of itself."

After she'd easily won the race, I thought the pressure would be off. But I was wrong. Evelyn ate very little and went straight to the room she shared with Karin. Later that evening she came hunting for me.

"I want to go home. Tonight," she told me as we walked back to her room.

That floored me, especially after what she'd said about needing money. I reminded her of the World Cup. "You can't run against Koch if you don't win the two hundred tomorrow."

"I don't care. I hate track. Will you take me to the airport?" Evelyn was already packed.

"Evelyn, is something wrong at home?"

She didn't answer my question. Instead, she firmly said, "I'm going home. I just have to go."

"Evelyn, I know how you feel."

"You don't know how I feel!" she snapped.

"But I do. It's normal for an athlete to ask herself, 'What the hell am I doing here?'—especially if there is some pressing matter at home. I remember asking the same question myself at the Tokyo Olympics. There was a bridge that connected the warm-up track to the stadium. I stood sweating and shaking on that bridge, waiting to start my first event, telling myself I didn't have to compete. I could go home instead, go skin diving with my husband instead of wondering what he was doing."

Evelyn was listening.

"Unfortunately, I had no coach or anyone else to talk to and calm me down. I was the only American pentathlete, so I had to argue with myself. The bridge seemed twenty miles long. Yes, I do know how you feel."

Evelyn sat down on the bed. The wrinkles were fading from her forehead.

"Remember what you told reporters who asked you about your comeback from the injury and disappointments of 1980? You said your body brought you back. All right, now your body's so ready to run, you'll sprint the fastest two hundred of your life. Your opponents will be so far back, they'll barely be able to see the soles of your spikes. You're a professional now. In show business they say 'The show must go on.' Well, in track the bang of the gun waits for no one." Glancing at one of Evelyn's half-finished novels on the nightstand, I said, "The only thing you have to worry about is will the handsome prince get his girl?"

She smiled, "How did you know there was a prince?"

"Isn't there always? And you'll be the queen tomorrow. Queen Victorious."

She was, too, in the beige sleeveless bodysuit. No one else came close.

In the beige suit Evelyn demonstrates perfect form. In Sacramento she again won the double.

In a few weeks we would be off to Europe for the summer circuit that led up to the World Cup in Rome. But now Evelyn and Karin (who'd won the javelin, as usual) and I rode south in the van, laughing at stories of the good old days at UCLA. We laughed, remembering Evelyn's painful contortions when she'd got her first case of bootie lock. We split our sides as Karin recalled the time she almost speared Tyrone Thompson with her javelin. Then Karin told us a story about Evelyn that surprised us both.

"I remember going with some friends to see the movie *Rocky* during our freshman year at UCLA. There was a girl with an Afro seated in front of me. The audience was silent as Rocky tried to get up the courage to kiss his girlfriend. Then the girl with the Afro shouted, 'Go for it. I'd kiss him.' " Karin was now looking directly at Evelyn. "Wasn't I shocked when I saw that girl coming out of the movie? It was the shy Evelyn Ashford."

We laughed and laughed, until we picked up my son Bradley in Santa Cruz. He came aboard with a six-foot boa constrictor coiled around his neck. The snake was a gift from his father, my ex-husband Jim Winslow. Evelyn looked at the boa with petrified eyes but didn't complain. After her victories she was in a mood to soothe me for a change. She knew I hated snakes but saw that Brad was determined to keep his boa. "Pat, it will be okay."

She took over the wheel and drove us home along the winding, dangerous Pacific Coast Highway. That allowed me to keep my eyes on old beady eyes, who was now wrapped around a branch in the cracked aquarium Brad had brought along to house it.

American track stars love to compete in Europe. In Viareggio, Nice, Zurich, West Berlin, Cologne, Koblenz, Brussels, and many other cities, they are as popular as baseball players are in America. Young and old pack the large stadiums for the competition, then follow the winners back to hotels, clamoring for autographs. Some fans sit up all night with their elaborate autograph books hoping to catch elusive stars sneaking in after parties. Fans also bring glossy photos to be autographed. (These are their answer to our baseball cards.)

Evelyn was adored by European track fans that summer of '81. They gazed at her. They smiled. Their remarks were kind and flattering, and in English so Evelyn could understand. They gave her flowers, candy, T-shirts, sport pins to trade, and expensive souvenirs like crystal vases or picture books. A young German girl gave us both some beautiful glossy photos of Evelyn wearing her black racing suit, which was a sensation in Europe. The girl wanted my autograph as the coach of the only sprinter to defeat the powerful East German women.

"Please, Evelyn. Please, coach. Sign this," people said everywhere we went.

Also milling around in hotel lobbies were club managers, trainers, doctors, coaches, track officials, shoe company representatives, and the wives, husbands, girlfriends, and boyfriends of the athletes. This "wolf pack" passed its time gossiping, making deals, and watching the large TV screens spaced around the hospitality room. Being shown were tapes of record performances in events from previous years. The tapes were played throughout the day until they were replaced with films of that day's competition.

"I hate the way I look when I run," said Evelyn before fleeing to her room to read. I remained, explaining to Ray the perfections and flaws I noticed in her and her competitors. I taught him about arm action, foot placement, knee lift, and body lean throughout the four stages of the race—start, acceleration, transition, and finish.

Like the partners of male athletes, Ray, I thought, often felt excluded from the excitement. With no races to run, no interviews to give, no autographs to sign, he was bored and wanted to go home to America. Evelyn wouldn't let him. She had her own private reasons for keeping him near. But I could see for myself how Ray helped to keep her loose in the pressure-cooker world of the circuit. He told hilarious tales of his childhood on the streets of

Detroit. His descriptions of characters he'd known, of dogs, criminals, and crimes in his old neighborhood, would often be just the right entertainment to ease Evelyn's tensions.

Ray kept his ear to the gossip pipeline too. He told us stories about athletes who were taking drugs. He hung out with the male athletes and listened to them brag about their shoe contracts and appearance deals. The inflated amounts he heard made him feel bad about Evelyn's meager earnings. He thought she was being ripped off by her shoe company.

"Pat Connolly doesn't know how to get big-time money for Evelyn," Ray was told by a coach who wanted to work with Evelyn. "You should find someone with more experience to negotiate for her."

I tried not to let this sort of talk get in the way of details that helped Evelyn's performance. My income was definitely tied to hers, and I needed every penny of it. In her speed suit Evelyn was running faster than ever before. She was getting more publicity for her new shoe sponsor than any other athlete, yet they did cheat, reneging on a $30,000 bonus they had promised her for wearing their racing suits. I finally agreed with Ray that we'd better change shoes.

I also agreed with Ray that Evelyn needed a professional agent. I was more concerned about her performances than the money she won for them. But whom could we trust?

I didn't know it at the time, but under my management Evelyn actually was one of the highest-paid women on the circuit. No wonder so many other coaches were trying to get her away from me. They saw her as a gold mine—for themselves, not the Olympic gold that I was striving for Evelyn to get.

CHAPTER TWELVE

Shoe Wars

The long European circuit was over and we were now in Rome waiting for the World Cup to begin. I had to settle Evelyn's shoe situation with RIO. When I told them we'd change shoes if they didn't keep their promise, the top RIO representative, a German with a booming voice, replied, "We'll destroy Evelyn. We'll sue her into the poorhouse. We'll use all our power to stop promoters from inviting her to meets."

I stood toe to toe with him, responding, "You'll make RIO look bad to all the other athletes. They won't trust you or wear your shoes again."

"Your little *schwarze* does not have that much influence."

Schwarze, a German word for "black," also has the slang meaning of "nigger." Infuriated by the racist German, I stormed away saying, "You're disgusting. Evelyn will never run in your shoes again."

Cubie Seegobin, the PUMA-USA representative, quickly made a deal with us right on the balcony of my hotel room in Rome. Cubie's competent manner impressed me, and Ray liked him too. Evelyn stayed out of the negotiations with "this shoe business," as she disgustedly called it. She felt uncomfortable talking to outsiders about money. But she was happy to hear about the large fee PUMA would be paying that would take care of her through the 1984 Olympics in Los Angeles.

"What's the verdict? What shoes do I wear tomorrow?" she asked in a flat voice when I went back to her room.

"PUMAs. The company is flying several pairs down from Germany first thing in the morning. I hope they fit. Here's the money."

I counted six thousand dollars in hundreds and fifties, a down payment on the new agreement. I had asked for cash because I didn't trust checks. Evelyn figured out my ten percent and handed it to me. I tucked it into my bra, because my pockets were already stuffed full with one-hundred-dollar bills we had earned on the circuit. My bustline got bigger traveling in Europe, for I never felt comfortable leaving money in our hotel rooms, and a purse was too easily forgotten or stolen.

Sports Illustrated had rented a Fiat for us to use while we were in Rome. Neither Evelyn nor Ray could drive a standard transmission, and Ray really preferred to hang out in the hotel or nearby shops rather than sightsee. To make sure Evelyn didn't sit around and stew about her upcoming competition, I drove her to the Vatican to marvel at the *Pietà* and the Sistine Chapel. Michelangelo's famous ceiling was being restored, and watching the painters working flat on their backs on high scaffolding, Evelyn wondered, "How did he have the patience? I get bootie lock, but he must have gotten body lock."

We shopped near the Spanish Steps, indulged ourselves with *gelati*, the creamier-than-American ice cream, and drank *aqua minerale* in the outdoor bars of the Via Veneto, leaving the *vino* to others. We drove around the old Colosseum and the ruins of the Forum. Later I suggested we drive outside the ancient walls of Rome to explore the Catacombs, but Evelyn said, "No way. Graves in caves and skeletons are not for me."

"How would you like to learn how to drive a stick shift?"

"Sure, why not?"

I drove us to a less congested part of the city. We traded places in the Fiat, tightened our seatbelts, and jerked down the street as Evelyn tried to let out the clutch at the same time she pressed the gas pedal. There were pedestrians crossing everywhere. "Go that way," I urged, seeing an unpaved side road.

"You'll get us lost."

"This must be the city dump. You can't hurt anything here."

Evelyn eyed a gang of ragged, dirty boys beginning to run toward our car. True competitor that she was, doing her best under pressure, she drove us away faster than a race-car driver. "You make me feel like we're on the *I Love Lucy* show. I'm Ethel and you're Lucy Ricardo, always getting us into an adventure." Back at the Villa Pamphilli, our hotel, Ray came to dinner with a present for Evelyn. He had gone off on his own to buy her a Gucci bag. She kissed his cheek.

The next morning, race day, as I paced the lobby awaiting the arrival of Evelyn's PUMAs, I caught sight of a RIO rep. He was trying to stay out of sight behind a fat marble piller. I had a creepy feeling he was spying on me and on hurdler Edwin Moses, who was also switching to another shoe. The competition between companies was ruthless. I remembered how RIO had played dirty when a rep of theirs had falsely tipped off customs in Mexico City during the '68 Olympics, claiming that a load of contraband would be coming in the PUMA shipment. When the PUMA-USA rep went to pick up his shoes, he was arrested and jailed for days until all the boxes were searched.

Yes, I had to be careful to save Evelyn from stress brought on by these shoe wars. I went back to my room to phone Cubie. "Your shoes are late,"

I told him. "Not only that, but your competitor has a man stationed down in the lobby."

"Evelyn's shoes met some problems on the way to the airport in Germany."

"Problems?"

"A car accident."

Goose bumps broke out on my arms. "Was anyone hurt?"

"I'm not sure. But Evelyn should have her shoes in an hour, from our factory in Switzerland. There will be a police escort to help us."

Along with these shoe pressures we had problems with Evelyn's USA team uniform. Her issued shorts were so big that they'd have fit a hippopotamus, and a smaller pair had not yet been delivered as promised. Because rules of competition specifically stated that athletes must wear their official team uniform, Evelyn wouldn't be allowed to compete in an outfit of her own choice. Panicked, I phoned the U.S. team manager, my old friend Willye White. "Evelyn's the only American woman who'll win three events here in Rome, yet she has no shorts to wear."

"Girl, calm down. I went shopping for some shorts that look like the uniform, and I have matching ribbon for stripes. I'm sewing it on now." As Willye had so many times in the past when we were both on U.S. teams, she saved the day for me.

Reliable, very handsome, and dressed like a movie

star, Cubie delivered the new PUMAs to us in Evelyn's room, and bingo, they fit. But by the time her shorts appeared, it was too late for her to take the team shuttle bus to the stadium. I had to drive her in the Fiat. I insisted she wear her old flats to the stadium, to fool the sneaky RIO rep who was spying on us as we crossed the hotel lobby. We would keep the shoe gangs guessing until Evelyn appeared on the track, first in her old spikes to warm up, then in her PUMAs to race.

Shoes! Shorts! The unexpected drive through unpredictable Roman traffic! Seeing Evelyn walking through the stadium tunnel onto the track, I felt safe at last—that is, until I noticed a photographer with a long lens rushing up to snap pictures of her. He stood in her lane, hindering her ability to take practice starts. Then, after he'd been moved to the infield by a track official, he again leaned into lane one, Evelyn's assigned lane. An alarm went off in my head: The man was close enough to Evelyn to distract her or possibly injure her.

I was too far away to yell at him or Evelyn, and I could find no one from the U.S. delegation to warn her.

"*Ai vostri posti.*" The starter called the runners to their marks.

The photographer barely stepped on the infield but continued to lean into Evelyn's lane. Was he there to hinder Evelyn? Evelyn herself seemed oblivious, in the same state of concentration she'd

When striving for world records, measured in hundredths of a second, the start becomes an exact science. Here I precisely measure Evelyn's blocks and make tapes she can take with her to the starting line. Tony Duffy/Allsport

achieved at the '76 trials. Normally such concentration was a good sign. Today I hoped she'd wake up to the danger.

I thought of leaping the moat to the track and tackling the photographer.

There was no time. The gun blasted. Instinctively Evelyn swerved out of lane one to avoid his big camera, but even with that wasted time it was obvious she'd win the race. She was flying around the turn, flying down the straightaway and across the finish line in a new meet record, a time that might well have been faster without a telephoto lens sticking in her lane.

Riding back to the hotel, Evelyn told me, "I didn't see any photographer or anything else."

Ray asked me, "Do you really think someone could've done that to Ash?"

"We'll never know" was all I could answer. The shoe negotiations and their aftermath had put me on edge. I drove back to the hotel the whole way building a head of steam. In the parking lot I blew up. "I've had it with this crap," I bellowed.

"What do you want? How much more money do I have to pay you?" Evelyn had completely misinterpreted my anger.

Slipped blocks are no excuse in a race so I tested Evelyn's before she ran. I noticed the holes were drilled in the wrong place. Notice Bob Hersh, the voice of the Olympics, and the East German coach carefully watching me.

"I've had it with all this money stuff getting in the way of your performances, Evelyn." With that outburst I began emptying my pockets, throwing hundred-dollar bills at her. Soon my ten percent of her PUMA money blew around her feet.

"Pat, stop it! What are you doing?"

"Money, money, money. Ray's constantly talking to everyone about money. Money's taking over this relationship." When I saw Ray picking up the bills I'd flung, I stopped and ran to my room. I wanted to go home. I called Harold for solace, and though he was thousands of miles away, he sounded close by, right there with me. "Why should I spend weeks away from my family only to deal with hassles about money? It's become an obsession with Ray and Evelyn."

"Her racing is her livelihood. They have a right to worry about how much she makes." As usual, Harold saw both sides of the problem.

"But Ray is listening to all the bull this wolf pack tells him over here. Can't he see that the leeches are using him to upset me and get to Evelyn?"

"Leeches are a part of our sport now. Times have changed, and so must you or forget coaching. Evelyn's a professional now. You've got to be professional too."

Harold was right but I kept talking. "I don't make enough money to be called professional. The other coaches don't do half of what I do for Evelyn and they're putting money in the bank. All mine goes for baby-sitting. I want more than chump change out of coaching. I want respect."

"Get Evelyn through her hundred-meter race tomorrow. Then you'll have the time to work out the money thing when you all get home."

Suddenly feeling alone and lonely, I cried out, "I wish you were here."

"We all miss you and love you very much. I'll be waiting at the airport the day after tomorrow."

I had to be the one to patch things up in Rome. I went to the Washingtons' room and told them, "We can't let anything destroy the preparation we've made for tomorrow's race. We'll solve our personal problems in California. Now let's go to dinner."

"OK."

We laughed over Ray's Detroit stories with our pasta that evening. Next day Evelyn was far from her psychological best but she won her race anyway. She also anchored the relay team to a new American record. A Double-Triple World Cup Champ.

On the long flight home I tried to come to grips with what was happening. I had three relationships with Evelyn: coach to athlete, manager to athlete, and friend to friend. I could see the day when she wouldn't need me as a manager or coach, but I didn't want to end our friendship.

CHAPTER THIRTEEN

Grand Prix

"I am sick of track," Evelyn grouched on the phone to me a few weeks after we'd returned from Rome. "If I have to run one more shake-up, I'll throw up."

"You *do* need a break. We both do." The thought of a vacation after six years of coaching Evelyn appealed to me that busy morning when I had already taken three-year-old Shannon along to Adam's soccer game and then to Bradley's basketball practice. "Evelyn, you can use your time to finish school. You should put your college diploma ahead of everything else." This was true but also a cop-out. Not wanting to think about the issue of our changing relationship and our friction over money, I found a good way to point Evelyn away from the track without discussing the tough problems.

There was silence from Evelyn.

"Well, Ash, if you and Ray still want to have a baby, this is a good time to take a break. I'll reassure PUMA that you'll be better than ever and they'll keep you on contract."

"You don't have to worry about PUMA. I've got an attorney who will handle that now. He's the man I introduced you to in Chicago last February. He must be good—he handles Magic Johnson."

I was relieved that she had someone to handle those things, so why was I taking her statement as a rebuff?

Trying not to let that show, I quickly continued. "All women athletes I have known, from Fanny Blankers to Wilma, have set personal records after giving birth. I did it myself after Bradley was born."

"Sounds good to me. Ray wants a family too."

Evelyn seemed momentarily happy with my suggestion for her break from running. But her leave lasted only until December, when she heard that Mobil Oil and Jean Naté were each sponsoring grand prix where she might win a whopping $30,000 by running eight indoor sixty-yard dashes the winter of 1982. The rules of track and field were changing. An athlete could now take money openly for competing.

"How can you expect me to take the year off when I can make so much money in just two months of running?" Evelyn protested.

She asked me to coach her again. We were spending less time together as friends; she'd gotten a new manager. I was relieved that at least she wanted me for a coach.

"I'll do it if you'll enroll in two classes. A college education will insure your future when you can't run any longer. I couldn't bear to see you end up on food stamps and welfare like other great athletes I've known."

We agreed. Evelyn would enroll in school during spring quarter, right after the Mobil Grand Prix. She'd been the top sprinter in the world since 1979 and fully expected to beat Alice Brown, Jeanette Bolden, and Florence Griffith handily. Coached by Bob Kersey, these women, though virtually the same age as Evelyn, were more rapidly improving and were gunning for her.

Alice had the most heart and talent of the lot, but I told Evelyn that Alice's legs were too short for her to be much of a threat. Jeanette, much taller than Evelyn, ran too upright, overstriding and looking more like a drum major than a sprinter. As for Florence, we'd all laughed when Ray named her the "Rocking Horse" because she rocked jerkily from side to side, a clear sign of weakness.

I was wrong about Jeanette. She shot out of the blocks like a man and won the first two races of the grand prix in January of '82. When I tried to console Evelyn, reminding her that she had been training only for two weeks, she burst into a fury. "I hate to lose to one of those monsters," she shrieked, using the wolf pack's name for Kersey's athletes.

"Kersey must have discovered some secret for power," I said, agreeing with Evelyn. It was tough to lose to athletes you normally had no problem beating. "Don't worry about them," I told Evelyn and myself. "The rhythm of your first steps out of the blocks isn't good yet. You aren't in shape either. Be patient. You can still win the grand prix."

The next weekend the thickly muscled Jeanette didn't show up in Toronto, but in Dallas she won again. She had used her unbelievable new strength to gain a big lead right out of the blocks.

"She beat you by only one hundredth of a second," I reminded Evelyn. At the next practice I had her concentrate on pushing both feet against the blocks in the set position. "You're still kicking up your back foot. You've got to keep it low to the ground as you punch your right knee forward. You also must pump your arms harder. They're strong now. Get them into the act."

Houston McTeer, who held the world record in the men's sixty, happened to be warming up in the lane next to ours at Drake Stadium during our last practice before the San Diego meet. With a little coaxing he agreed to take some starts with Evelyn. My spirits lifted in the warm, sage- and eucalyptus-scented Santa Ana winds that blew in the direction Evelyn and Houston were running. I felt that if Evelyn could get used to Houston's power out of the blocks, Jeanette's winning days were over. The heavily muscled McTeer knelt in the blocks next to the sylphlike Evelyn. With my gun they came out almost together. I wasn't surprised. Evelyn had been bench pressing 145 pounds, and her other weight exercises—her flies, inclines, and power tracks—had improved equally. Strong as she was, she still looked like a woman and weighed less than 120. Pound for pound she was as strong as Houston. She had taken pleasure in beating every football player who'd challenged her in other practices, but Houston was a trained sprinter, and Evelyn stayed within a meter of him for thirty yards.

Evelyn was ready for her last head-to-head race with Bolden and Brown before the final grand prix meet at the indoor championships in New York City. I asked the promoter to fly us to San Diego the day of the meet. We had had enough of hotels.

The old-fashioned biplane waiting for us at the gate made me wonder if the thing could be another *Spirit of St. Louis* and the pilot's name Charles Lindbergh. "The world's fastest woman in the slowest plane," I said as we taxied down the runway for what turned out to be a beautiful flight. Hugging the rugged California coastline at a low altitude, we watched our shadow gliding along the sapphire water. Only the twin domes of the San Onofre nuclear plant marred our view. "Tonight you'll run so fast, your fans will think you're nuclear powered." She liked to hear me talk that way

I once got Evelyn into A men's 50-meter race. Though Houston won (5:84) and Evelyn was last, the men's speed pulled her to a new American record. (The 6:26 time was disallowed because she had been "helped" by men.) AP/Wide World Photos

even though she knew such compliments were my not-so-subtle means of "psyching her up."

There were five runners in the women's 60-yard dash that night: Alice Brown, Jeanette Bolden, Diane Williams, a runner from Japan, and Evelyn.

I found an empty seat in the crowd and listened to people talk. They seemed more curious about what Evelyn Ashford would be wearing than about who would win. I could have bet them that she'd be in a blue-and-white-striped leotard with puff sleeves (we'd bought it at a boutique), but I had more fun listening.

"Isn't she a fox," said a man nearby. He whistled as Evelyn pulled off her sweats. He didn't notice that while waiting for this crucial race, I was sitting four inches above my seat.

Evelyn got out well and within five steps she was in first. With a sigh of relief I sat back to enjoy the race until I realized that Jeanette and Alice had stopped running. Watching them, I missed Evelyn's finish. But I didn't miss hearing the announcer yipping, "Ashford's unofficial winning time of 6.49 breaks the world record." Before I could bask in the satisfaction of her time, I saw Kersey approach and start to talk heatedly to Evelyn.

"Kersey wants to run it again. He's claiming a false start," the promoter explained when I'd reached him on the track.

I protested. "He should teach his athletes the rules of racing. Everyone knows you never stop in a race unless you hear the recall gun." I walked away to check with the starter and recall starter. Neither of them thought there had been a false start. I grabbed a confused Evelyn, saying, "Take off your spikes and warm down."

"But Kersey says we have to run the race over. If they do, I have to run. I need the grand prix points."

"He's wrong. You'll get your points." I guided Evelyn away, only to be followed by Kersey, a ranting bully by now. He cursed me loudly and raised his fists ready to punch whoever talked back to him.

"Get lost," I said right in his face. "You're out of control. All your yelling won't do your team any good. They're so poorly coached, they can't even figure out when to run and when to stop."

An official stepped between us just before Kersey's fist landed on my nose. I hurried out of the arena to a TV truck, where I watched Evelyn's race on the monitor. With the advantage of slow motion I could see that Jeanette had moved first from the blocks. Alice had gone with her. I also saw an instant replay of the crowd's astonishment when Kersey tried to punch me.

Next day in San Francisco, Mary Anne picked us up at the airport and gave us the sports pages that featured Evelyn's world-record win. Stories described Kersey's behavior, mine, the promoter's, and Evelyn's, adding that she'd been awarded her grand prix points, but not the world record, because of the controversy.

"Those starts with Houston McTeer really helped me," Evelyn decided while we ate lunch with Mary Anne, a vice-president of marketing and property development who was now becoming an expert in track-and-field. That night Evelyn took it easy but still won her race in San Francisco's Cow Palace, where the track had been built over a dusty, manure-filled rodeo floor. Jeanette and Alice hadn't come, allowing Evelyn to save her speed for their final rematch the following Friday in New York. Behind in points, she *had* to win there.

My Shannon, three, and Adam, six, went with us to New York. We all stayed in the Penta Hotel just across the street from Madison Square Garden, turning our connecting rooms into a cozy family center. I brought California fruit, nuts, and other food so we wouldn't have to eat every meal in expensive restaurants. We filled our trash cans with ice and juice from the hotel machines. Between snacks my kids jumped on the beds and clowned around with Ray as he listened to jazz tapes on his headset. He and Evelyn seemed to enjoy these shenanigans. I felt they'd be wonderful parents someday. Maybe someday soon!

Evelyn had not had her menstrual period for six weeks. She had never missed a period as long as I'd been coaching her. When I'd mentioned that she was probably pregnant, she'd seemed pleased. Now I teased, "Your baby is in for a fast ride tonight." We both felt the pressure of the coming race, for it would determine who'd win the prize money, who was the fastest American, and who was the best coach. Jeanette's heat time that morning had been two hundredths of a second faster than Evelyn's.

After stretching and icing Evelyn, I gave her and Ray a break by taking my boisterous kids out on the town. In bitter cold we walked over to see the

Empire State Building. We ate hot roasted pretzels and chestnuts sold by the street vendors. We shopped at Macy's. Then we returned to the room to pass the rest of the time watching cartoons. "Be quiet," I whispered. "Evelyn's sleeping.

But she wasn't. She slipped into my room and sat down on the bed. "Something's wrong," she mumbled. "I feel terrible."

I looked closely at her pale cheeks and terrified eyes. "What's the matter?" I asked.

"I have cramps. I'm bleeding."

"Oh, no. You may be having a miscarriage."

Within the next hour of quiet sobbing and painful cramps, Evelyn did have a miscarriage. I held on to her, saying, "I've miscarried before. It's nature's way of telling us everything isn't right this time. At least you know you can get pregnant. Remember Dr. K said you're the healthiest person he knows?

"We were so excited about having a baby," she sobbed.

"You'll have a baby when Mother Nature's time is right." I'd been looking forward to "coaching" her through her first pregnancy, to buying baby things with her, even to baby-sitting, but I didn't want to show my disappointment now.

"Come on, Ash, we can do it again." Ray, gentle and sensitive, knew better than anyone how to comfort his wife. I left them alone, Evelyn curled in a little ball with her eyes closed and Ray beside her.

Later I went into their room to say, "Only you

know how you feel about the race tonight. Evelyn, you don't have to run. You can go see the meet doctor if you want."

"I do have to run, I guess."

"Since you're in such excellent condition and your pregnancy wasn't very far along, I don't think you will hurt yourself if you do. But only if you've stopped bleeding. And if you promise to see your doctor when you get home."

My kids and I left for another walk. When we got back, Evelyn had moved to the floor and was stretching. "The baby's already lost," she said. "But my race can still be won." The heavy bleeding had subsided. She did shake-ups barefoot in the hall while Ray and I guarded the intersecting hallways. Only a few guests wandered past us with questioning looks. No questions were asked on our walk to the arena. In her layers of sweat suits, windbreakers, and a heavy overcoat to stay warm, Evelyn looked like a bag lady. Even so, people on Seventh Avenue recognized her, saying, "There's Ashford."

The race announcer made much of Evelyn's sixty-yard final. To excite the crowd he gave a long history of her accomplishments as well as those of Jeanette, Alice, Diane, and Chandra, all of whom were in the final.

If he only knew what she's just gone through, I told myself. *I shouldn't be letting her run.*

Meanwhile Kersey strutted in front of me, to

show he was confident his sprinters would be the best.

Jeanette got out just a little ahead of everyone. "RUUUUNNNNNNNN" I screamed to Evelyn for the rest of the race. Evelyn finally passed Jeanette just one meter from the photo-finish cameras. Evelyn's winning time set a new world record for the distance, a record that Kersey couldn't take away from her with lame excuses about false starts. Tears filled my eyes as I swung Evelyn around and around in a circle.

"Are you okay?" I croaked, my voice gone.

"I'm relieved."

Sweet revenge! After an agonizing afternoon, Evelyn comes back to beat Jeanette and break the world record. AP/Wide World Photos

CHAPTER FOURTEEN

In the Heat of the Fight

Evelyn's mind was made up. She wanted a million dollars. She wanted a big house, an expensive car, and the finest clothes. She wanted fame and glory, neither of which would come from being a college student.

"What if you break a leg in a car accident and can never compete again?"

Evelyn nearly took my head off with her answer. "You just stick to coaching! You can't tell me how to live my life!"

I had tried to compartmentalize the different roles we had in our relationship: sometimes concerned friends, most times mentor and student. Evelyn saw no separation. I was only her coach, her overly intrusive coach. Husband, sisters, in-laws, accountants, and attorneys all put pressures on Evelyn that ultimately depended on her track performances; but by December of '82 they were none of my concern. I tried to look at the situation dispassionately, but tears kept welling up in my eyes.

Mary Anne, who had spent a lot of time with Evelyn, helped me by saying, "You and Evelyn have grown so close that she feels like a daughter who must sever the apron strings from a domineering mother."

"Yet she asks for my help with her private life so often," I protested.

"Can't you see she's behaving like your son Bradley? One moment he wants Mom to butt out of all his decisions and the next he needs you for every little problem he faces."

A light went on! I remembered how I shared with Evelyn the ups and downs of Brad's own rebellion. She listened with a sympathetic ear, yet she defended Brad's urges to break away.

"You're right," I told Mary Anne. "My seventeen-year-old son and my twenty-four-year-old athlete want to make their own choices in life. But—but still, it's terrible for Evelyn to give up on her college education."

I stopped counseling her after that, stopped insisting on many things, but not on the privacy of our training sessions. Evelyn's growing entourage and the press were definitely banned from Drake, as was all talk of racing for money only. We set our goals for the coming season: to break the 100-meter world record and to win the World Championship in '83. As for Evelyn's own personal goal of making a million dollars, it might well result from winning a gold medal in the '84 Olympics. The endorsements alone could give her security for life. But what if she broke a leg instead?

Her competitors were not going to lie down and roll over either. East Germans still held and were improving their world outdoor records. Russian sprint times were coming down (Soviet star Kondrateyva had defeated Gohr to win the Olympic Gold in Moscow). Tall Jamaican Merlene Ottey clearly had the graceful long stride to beat Evelyn. And among the Americans, Chandra had been making a comeback with the help of a new coach. The coach who'd tried to get me to use drugs had been pumping quick-footed Diane Williams full of steroids, saying, "Take these pills. It's the only way you can beat Ashford." Young, and trusting her coach, Diane went along with his program until she noticed alarming changes in her body. And Kersey continued to groom a stableful of women to dethrone Evelyn.

Unruffled by talk of her competition, Evelyn gave her best effort to our twice-a-day training sessions. Occasionally she ran 10 kilometers worth of 100-meter fast shake-ups—that is, a hundred of them! Not even Elliot Mason could keep up with her. Joan Benoit, later to win the '84 Olympic marathon, watched my athletes with amazement. "I never

We tossed a heavy rubber medicine ball to gain dynamic strength. Evelyn gave up on having long finger nails which broke to the quick from my hard passes. B. B. Winslow

Jumping up Drake Stadium stairs was just one of many drills for Evelyn. The camera angle here makes her legs look much shorter than they really are.

realized that sprinters work so hard. Their workouts last longer than mine, and I'm training for a twenty-six-mile race."

"You're right Joan, and tonight they have another hour of weight training."

In order for Evelyn to break a world outdoor record, the weather conditions had to be exactly right. Many of Evelyn's attempts had been hampered by wind: a head wind slamming into her face or a crosswind blowing her nearly into the next lane, or a wind at her back that gave her extra speed but made her times "wind aided" so they didn't go into the record book. "Mother Nature has been kind to you," I always said to encourage Evelyn on windy days. "She's given you good health and talent and she's now using wind to make you work."

"*I am working,*" Evelyn would announce after yet another race spoiled by wind.

"Be patient. When you least expect it, the record will come."

Evelyn was invincible the indoor season of 1983. And she easily won the 100 and 200 at the TAC Outdoor Nationals in Indianapolis the following June, though Chandra and Diane were getting closer. There were now three big meets ahead of us before I would turn her loose with Ray to make money on the European circuit that year: a dual meet with the East Germans in the Los Angeles Coliseum; the U.S. Olympic Sports Festival in Colorado Springs at the Air Force Academy; and the World Championships to be held in Helsinki, at Finland's Olympic Stadium.

Koch and Gohr were in Evelyn's hometown. Before the DDR-versus-USA meet in the prerace warm-up area, Evelyn noticed that the East Germans looked away or tried to avoid her entirely. "The

East Germans never look me in the eye. What's wrong with them?"

Evelyn used her own eyes with great force and expression. I could only guess an answer. "If I were your competitor, I wouldn't want to look you in the eyes either. Your looks can kill. Besides, the DDR sports psychologists have probably trained their runners to pretend you don't exist off the track. In the same way, I want you to wear imaginary blinders while you are running. Think of no one. See no one. By the way, I expect their coach to put both of them in the hundred to divide your focus."

As it happened, the East Germans didn't need a plot to steal Evelyn's focus. She was already distracted by tension with Ray. Not wanting to pry, I said nothing, but maybe I should have. Evelyn's form came apart in her race. Lacking concentration, she was slow out of the blocks and then panicked trying to catch up. She began overstriding, the same mistake she'd made as a beginner but not since. With her extra-long strides throwing her off balance, her arms began to flail. She didn't catch Gohr and barely beat Koch and Williams.

"I disgraced myself in front of my hometown crowd," Evelyn wailed when I finally found her in the corner of an empty bathroom.

"You've got another chance in forty minutes to beat Gohr, 'cause you'll both be anchoring the relay."

On her home turf, Evelyn gets whipped by Gohr, barely beating Koch and Williams. DDR vs. USA, 1983. Bill Leung

"It's not the same on a relay."

"Evelyn, I'm not sure what your trouble is, but as your coach I can tell you that a true professional athlete leaves her family problems home. You brought yours with you today."

"You're right."

"Then for now don't think about anything but the relay. The team is counting on you."

When I returned to my seat in the stands, I told Mary Anne, who'd brought her nieces down for the meet, "We'll beat the East Germans by more than a meter."

"I'll bet five dollars on Gladish, Wockel, Koch, and Gohr," said a fat, pugnacious man sitting behind us.

"I wouldn't steal your money. Look at the fire on Ashford's face. I feel sorry for poor Gohr."

Alice Brown, Diane Williams, and Chandra Cheeseborough ran so fast that the American team led when Evelyn got the baton. The porker behind us cried, "Son of a beehive," as Evelyn beat Gohr by more than two meters.

All hell broke loose the next day. Evelyn phoned to say she was leaving Ray. "I don't know where I'm going," she murmured. The distress in her voice tore at my heart.

"Come over to my house," I said in a steady voice. "We'll talk if you want to." I waited on my porch until Evelyn's car screeched into the driveway. She was shaking, crying. In my living room she punched the couch with both hands. I immediately removed my coaching hat and let the deep concern I felt take over.

"Did Ray do something?"

"What didn't Ray do? He blames me because I'm always away at track practice or meets. I don't want to talk about it. I just don't want to talk about it!"

I said nothing more. Later I drove Evelyn over to spend the night with a friend in case Ray came looking for her at my house. Then I pleaded with

Revenge of the relay. Here the talented and powerful Chandra Cheesborough hands off to Evelyn. The East Germans didn't have a chance. DDR vs. USA, 1983. K. S. Photos

Elliot. "You've got to help them." He had counseled the Washingtons in the past. Now he would have to work his magic again to save their marriage.

It was fortunate that he was at practice the next day, because when Evelyn came out to jog, she started running each lap faster and faster. She wouldn't stop. The swollen-faced sprinter who hated long distance was out of control and on the way to her third mile when I wrestled her to the ground. "You don't have to practice today. Please go somewhere with Elliot and talk this thing out."

Counseling both Ray and Evelyn, Elliot was eventually able to get them to work out their problems, but not before Evelyn reluctantly had to go off to Colorado Springs for the Olympic Sports Festival and the World Championships in Helsinki. The starting pistol waits for no one.

"I don't want to go to the Sports Fest, but Elliot thinks I should. It will give him time to talk with Ray. But Pat, I don't feel like competing."

"You didn't feel like taking those thousands of starts you've taken the past eight years. Nor running in the waves when you couldn't swim. Nor tossing a heavy medicine ball. Nor doing a trillion shake-ups and bench presses. But you did them anyway. You've done everything for speed and you are in the best shape of your life. Just go to Colorado. A change of scene might help you think more clearly."

"I guess."

When she arrived at the airport in Colorado

Springs, Evelyn phoned to say she'd decided not to run. "Go warm up anyway and see how you feel then."

When she arrived at the Air Force Academy, she phoned again to tell me there were too many clouds and too much wind to run. "I'm not going to run."

"No one can make you run, but you *need* to run. It will help you get some of the frustration you are feeling out of your system. Don't worry about anything. Just run."

"I don't know," she said, and hung up.

Two hours later my phone rang again.

"Pat, this is Evelyn."

"I know your voice."

"I broke the world record. I ran ten seventy-nine, and the wind was legal. I was still hysterical about everything, so I didn't care if I won or lost. I just ran recklessly. I practically cried the whole race."

"Hurry back. We all love you."

"There is nothing to come back to."

"Then change your ticket to San Francisco. You can rest and relax by the pool at the Saylers' house in Woodside. I'll meet you there. We'll forget about track and our husbands for a few days. Mary Anne will take us to the city for shopping and to the coast for crab cioppino."

"Okay."

FOLLOWING PAGE:
Actual photo from the automatic timer of Evelyn's world record.   Accutrack

EVELYN ASHFORD
WORLD RECORD 100 meters
10.79 seconds
July 3, 1983
National Sports Festival
U.S. Air Force Academy
Colorado Springs, Colorado
Phototime by ACCUTRACK

CHAPTER FIFTEEN

Trials and Tribulations

In July, at her last track workout before we left for the World Championships in Finland, Evelyn ran four fifty-meter sprints against one of Coach Bush's male quarter milers. She won all of them with her fastest times ever. Just as she was slowing down from her final sprint of the day, several children wandered onto the track in front of her, and she had to swerve abruptly to avoid crashing into them. At top speed her muscles weren't ready for a sudden change of direction, and she felt a searing pain in her bootie.

Ice, I thought, and hurried to get it.

The tear in Evelyn's gluteus maximus did not heal. She was not able to practice handoffs with the relay team, and it still hurt a week later as she warmed up for the first round of heats in Helsinki. I would have taken her out of most other competitions to make certain that she didn't injure the muscle further, but this was the World Championships. I left the choice to Evelyn: "You don't have to run injured. I'll explain to the American team coaches and the press how you were hurt last week."

"No way! I don't care how much it hurts, I won't chicken out of a big meet like this," she insisted. Rumors were flying around the championships about her injury. No one expected her to win even her first heat, yet she did, and in a time that gave notice to the East Germans. They couldn't afford to write off Ashford. At the entrance of the 1952 Olympic Stadium in Helsinki stood a statute of Paavo Nurmi, a great Finnish runner who had won race after grueling race with what the Finns call "SISU." SISU describes the valor that the Finns exhibited in defending their country from an invading Soviet army in 1939. Evelyn too, was running with "SISU."

As a result of random seeding Ashford and Gohr were together in the second round of heats. Evelyn won with a time of 11.11 to Gohr's 11.16, but I noticed as Evelyn cautiously slowed down at the end of the race that she was in pain. Her gluteus was tearing a little more with each race.

Once again I offered to scratch her from the meet.

"I am going to run, no matter what. My marriage is breaking, my bootie is breaking. The only thing I can do with myself is run."

"Okay, but please go as slowly as you can and still qualify for the final. You don't have to prove anything in the semi."

She did run easily but faster yet, 10.99. Gohr's winning semi was 11.08. Koch's times had been only hundredths slower. The final came about an hour later, and the entire track-and-field world was watching the rematch of these three fierce competitors, but any of the finalists listed on the scoreboard could win it all: Ashford—USA; Gohr—DDR; Koch—DDR; Ottey—JAM; Williams—USA; Brown—USA; Baily—CAN, and Gladish—DDR.

Reporters clamored for information about Evelyn's injury. I had already spoken with *Sports Illustrated*'s Anita Verschoth and Kenny Moore. I hoped they would do a cover story on Evelyn. "She's doubled in two World Cups and broken world records indoors and out," I said. "You've put Mary Decker's face on your cover for less than that. What do Evelyn and other black women like Wilma Rudolph, Wyomia Tyus, and Cheryl Miller [the great USC basketball player] have to do for the same treatment?"

Kenny answered. "My guess is that our editors don't believe that a black woman on the cover will sell magazines."

Rather than explode in a rage at yet another

example of racism in the sports world, I bit my tongue. I asked Anita and Kenny, "Just when are your editors going to recognize women for their athletic performances and stop looking at their figures and color? Why do they demand that we be pleasing to men? At *S.I.* you ignore women all year and then come out with that bathing suit issue you do. Is that your editors' idea of athletic women?"

Such talk was chalked up to "Crazy Connolly," as was my slap at *Track and Field News*, whose expert Stan Eales had predicted (even before the injury) that Gohr would beat Ashford in the final. I had noticed over the years that when the odds were even, *TAF News* seemed to favor white athletes. I pointed this out to an editor, who immediately told me I was "absurd" and brushed off my suggestions for fair-minded coverage of black athletes. Yet I had overheard them talking to each other and to some of the experts, saying that the World Championships final with Ashford versus Gohr would be a classic confrontation: black versus white, West versus East.

To me, the "classic" in confrontation would mean the showdown between a scientifically trained robot and a natural artist. Accusations about Evelyn's success being drug induced were circulating. With no way to prove otherwise, we at least needed to prove to ourselves, to Harold, and to other women athletes who believed we were "clean" that victories were possible—without steroids.

The tear in Evelyn's muscle was getting so large I could feel its depression with my own fingers. Thinking about it brought giant tears of frustration down my face as the runners were called to their marks. At last the gun cracked. Evelyn was just a hair behind Gohr at 50 meters. I stopped crying, thinking Evelyn had already won because her acceleration over the second 50 meters had always been the fastest. But the shreds that were left of her muscle couldn't stand the strain of her sudden shift of gears. It snapped, and with it her hamstring muscle. At full speed, she went down hard on the track,

Evelyn is carried off the track by medics.   AP/Wide World Photos

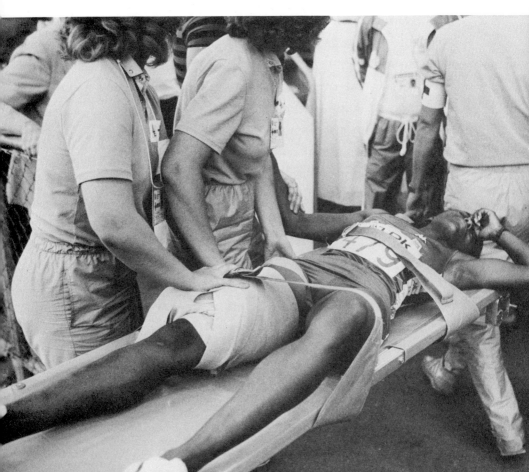

and Gohr went on to win in a slow 11.08. Koch came in second, and Williams third.

The medics helped me take her to the first-aid room under the stands, where the Finnish doctors tried to examine her. They put ice only on her hamstring, not realizing that her bootie was injured also. They looked at me strangely as I put ice on her butt. I didn't care what they thought; I had never seen Evelyn in such agony before. I knew the pain was more than physical. Wrapped into each uncontrollable sob was injured pride, despair about her marriage, and her lost chance to make more than $50,000 on the upcoming European circuit.

Harold had joined me in Helsinki. We had planned a second honeymoon in Finland after I sent Evelyn on to the European meetings. But now he suggested we fly back to Los Angeles with Evelyn. "She's in too much pain to face the long flight alone."

In L.A. I did leave her alone to face her problems with Ray. When she finally called me in October, just nine months from the '84 Olympic Games, she sounded much, much better and she was ready to train. She said, "Ray is coaching basketball at a junior college near Palm Springs. We've made it through our first five years of marriage. The rest should be easy."

"Marriage is never easy. I should know," I said. "But I'm happy for you, Evelyn. We can't train at

Drake anymore because the track is being resur-
faced. Cal State L.A. has a good track, and it's
closer to your new house in Pomona. We'll run
there and do our weight training two times a week
in Santa Monica. George [the owner of the Santa
Monica Body Building Center] has built us the hang-
ing leg-raise bars I've requested."

George's gym had become home for Sylvester
Stallone, so Evelyn now trained with her movie
idol, Rocky. He grew interested in her routine, no-
ticing the great strength in the small woman. When
he saw her press a 55-pound dumbbell in each hand
on the incline bench, then bench press 155 pounds,
then repeatedly hoist over 600 pounds on the ram
rack, Rocky himself was knocked out.

Yet Evelyn complained one day after practice,
"I'm not working hard enough. I should be doing
more. This is the year I *have* to win."

"The biggest mistake an athlete can make in an
Olympic year is to train too hard. I am keeping
your workouts easy for two reasons: First, I want
to make certain that your injuries are properly
healed. Second, I have planned that this season
would be easier. You have paid your dues in hard
workouts all these years. You won't be too tired
from practice to decorate your new home with
Ray." Her new PUMA contract had helped her
fulfill her dream of owning her own house.

Cubie Seegobin from PUMA purchased a $2,000
electronic timing device for me called Audo Start.

With its infrared sensors accurately timing each ten-meter section to the hundredth of a second, I learned that Evelyn was mentally drifting—not fully concentrating—from the 20-meter mark to 50 meters. Watching videotapes of her past races, I could see that the East Germans had made the same analysis of Evelyn and had trained their sprinters to put the pressure on her in those 30 meters. Evelyn caught on to what I taught her about rhythm and concentration and soon found herself flying so fast that we both were afraid she'd lose her balance.

"That thing you're making me do really works. But Pat, it is scary to run so fast."

"Remember the definition of sprinting that I told you several years ago? Sprinting is overcoming the fear of falling. Now you know what I mean."

Evelyn was excited. "This is our secret."

"Sure. We'll call it *the thing*."

"Don't tell anyone else about what we are doing."

"OK, but we have to be careful not to use *the thing* except for special occasions, because every muscle in your body is so finely tuned—stretched to the max and contracting with such force—that the least distraction could cause an injury."

By the time of the trials in June of 1984, we knew the Eastern European countries and their allies would boycott the '84 Olympics to get even with the U.S. for its boycott of the '80 Games in Moscow. We also knew our American women athletes would find winning their events easier without competition from Russians, East Germans, Poles, Bulgarians, and others who had long dominated certain women's sports, including track-and-field. I was confident that Evelyn could win both the 100 meters and the 200 meters at the Olympics on the basis of her strength and competitive experience. She could save her top speed—*the thing*—for the biggest European meeting after the Games in Zurich, Switzerland. I asked the Zurich meet promoter to invite the East Germans so that Gohr, Koch, and Evelyn would get yet another chance to race.

But we had to go through the formality of making the U.S. Olympic Team, where no matter how many records you might hold, you have to be in the top three finishers. The trials are truly a "sudden death" track meet.

The first two rounds of the 100 meters were a cinch, and because the trials were right there in Los Angeles, Vicki Vodon was able to work with Evelyn before and after each heat. As in car racing, we were a team. I had designed Evelyn's racing machine, Evelyn had built it, and Vicki kept it tuned.

The practice track was at Southern California University, three quarters of a mile from the Los Angeles Coliseum, where the trials were taking place. After warming up for the 100-meter quarter final, Evelyn came over to me on the practice track to ask, "Should I try *the thing* in my race?

I told her, "No. You don't need it to win here."

"I'd like to see if I can still do it."

"Evelyn, be patient. You can try it in the Games and in Europe."

"But I'd just like to try it now."

"Oh well, go ahead. Just once before you catch the competitors' bus to the stadium."

I shouldn't have given in to Evelyn's pleas. She wasn't used to slowing down from the high speed she attained with *the thing*, and something popped behind her right knee as she decelerated. "I think I've hurt my leg again," she murmured as I walked up to her on the track.

"Where does it hurt?" I felt like someone had just socked me hard in the back.

"Just above my right knee."

"Let's get Vicki."

Evelyn lay on the table in the training tent face-down. Other athletes and coaches were staring at her, sensing something wrong with the world record holder. I whispered in Evelyn's ear, "Vicki's going to need time to tape your whole leg. Stay calm. You must lie there and reinvent the word 'positive.' You'll be OK. You're in the best hands. I'll find a car to drive us to the stadium." To myself I said, *No excuse of ours will keep the starter's gun from going off.* I dashed away, leaving Vicki working like a beaver, and I soon found a golf cart and a driver with security clearance to get us through the gates of the Coliseum. I rushed back to the tent to tell Vicki, "You'll have to finish taping Evelyn on the golf cart. We have only ten minutes. If she

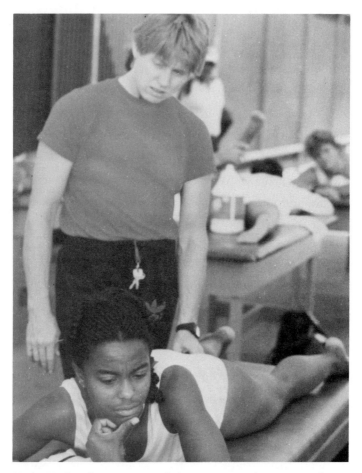

Vicki Vodon became one of the most popular trainers but she always had time for Evelyn.   Lynda Huey

misses the start, she misses the Olympics."

I had borrowed a pair of tights from another runner for Evelyn to wear so the tape wouldn't unravel or rub between her legs. (She'd never run with tape on her legs before.) Even at full throttle golf carts are slow, and when a truck blocked the only intersection we could go through, I jumped down to scream at the truck driver, *"Please move now. We're late to the Olympics. Nine years of our work are for nothing if we don't get there. Now!"*

The sheer desperation in my voice got the driver to inch forward and let us squeeze past his truck. The runners had already been called through the tunnel into the stadium to prepare their blocks. Vicki jogged along still applying the last piece of adhesive tape to Evelyn.

"Just qualify for the final, Evelyn. Don't run any faster than you have to. The first four qualify. Try to be third." I found a seat near the finish line, next to my old coach, Ed Parker. He rubbed my neck to calm me down. I remembered he'd always been there when I'd needed him. "Evelyn's injured." I started to say more but didn't have to talk. I could also communicate with *my* coach without words. Each athlete has her own ritual for the way she gets into her blocks on the starting line. I watched only Evelyn, trying to reassure myself from her movements that she would be OK. Did she shake out her back leg a little less vigorously than usual? Were her hips up too high in the set position? When the gun went off, I covered my eyes with my hands. "Tell me if she places in the top four."

"Her start was rough. She's off balance but she's moving into . . . third! Yes, she ran raggedly but she's safely qualified for the finals," Mr. Parker reassured me.

Vicki would now have time to use ice and stretch

In her own tights for the Olympic trials final, Evelyn again must run with "SISU." In the same way the camera focuses only on Evelyn, she has blocked everything from her mind but the finish line. Jeff Johnson

ing. She could properly wrap both of Evelyn's legs for balance. We had an hour and a half before the final. Time for me to hustle extra tape from the official Olympic trainers who didn't like Vicki's using their facility. "You can't take all that tape," one trainer said, trying to grab it from me. "It's for the athletes."

Pointing to Evelyn I retorted, "What do you think she is, a giraffe?"

Ray and Elliot had been watching the semifinal in the stands. Realizing that Evelyn had a problem with her leg, they jogged over from the stadium and found me on the practice track. Ray seemed shaken having seen his wife hobbling into third place. "What's wrong with Ash?" he asked abruptly as I snuck him and Elliot onto the warm-up track.

"Vicki thinks it's a small tear near the insertion of her hamstring, behind her knee."

"Will she be able to run the final?" Ray and Elliot asked together.

"Vicki's working on Evelyn with her magic hands. I believe she'll be okay."

At the trainer's tent Ray bent over to kiss his wife. She began to cry but stopped when Ray told her, "Ash, you can do it. You just always have to make things exciting." He hadn't lost faith in his delicate-looking but mentally tough wife.

Elliot held our hands and said a quiet prayer. Then we put Evelyn on the competitors' bus and we ran for the Coliseum. At the gates I shouted,

"Ray, you sit near the start and cheer. Elliot, you sit at the fifty-meter mark and pray. I'll sit on the finish line and hope. We'll be with Evelyn every step of the race."

Mr. Parker was still in the same seat. I ducked my head behind his shoulder, but this time I peeked with one eye as he called the race. "She's out with the pack. She seems okay. She's taking the lead. She's pulling away from Brown and Bolden. Sheeee's won it! With a meter to spare! Your girl is on the team." I looked up to see Evelyn with a huge smile walking back to the finish line. She also had a huge limp. Now with only five weeks to go before the Games, I'd really be tested as a coach.

CHAPTER SIXTEEN

Gold

By the time I got home, I didn't have the energy to lift my arms and open the door. The 500-pound gorilla was now on my back, and I hadn't sprinted a step. Harold was too absorbed with his son Jimmy's own attempt to make the Olympic team, in the decathlon, to help with my state of exhaustion.

Along with Evelyn's problems there was Michele Hopper's misfortune. She'd been training with me and Evelyn for four years, gradually improving her times in the 800 meters and 1500 meters. She had qualified for the trials in both races but wouldn't have a chance to make the team because she had contracted mononucleosis, a virus that sapped her strength for running. Yet as weak as she was, she still wanted to compete, leaving me to worry that she might seriously damage her health.

It broke my heart to watch her place last in her heat of the trials. Where was my luck? Evelyn had been injured. Michele had been struck with an illness no one can overcome in a short time. Jimmy had disastrous results in the long jump and discus and didn't make the team either, placing sixth. Karin barely made her third Olympic team, but watching her throw the javelin with bandages on practically every joint reminded me of her first office visit, when I'd told her, "You must also have some luck."

Such exhausting pressure at practice and at home had been causing me to neglect myself. My younger children needed their mother more than ever. My son Bradley had just graduated from high school and was being recruited to play college basketball. Helping him decide on a school, trying to be supportive of Jimmy's Olympic hopes, and attending Merja's volleyball games on her UCLA team left me with no energy for my own exercise. I gained twenty pounds and felt sick.

Dr. Krakovitz scolded me. "If you don't build up the iron in your blood, you won't be any good to your family or your athletes. Right now you are anemic."

I was further upset by Evelyn, who insisted on trying to make the Olympic team in the 200 meters.

"I have to run the two hundred! It's my favorite event."

"Why take the risk of more heats? We may not

have enough time as it is to rehabilitate your injury before the Games. If you rip it more, you're finished."

"I'm going to run, Pat."

"I can't believe you're going to jeopardize your chance for two gold medals!" I screamed, dizzy from the anemia and getting impatient with her. Evelyn did try to limp through the first round of the 200 heats but gave up five steps out of the blocks. I came down from the stands to console her. There would be no chance for a 200-meter gold medal.

"Evelyn, take a week off from training to give your leg a chance to heal. Be sure to see Vicki for treatments. In the meantime I have to figure out how I am going to have you ready for the Games, as well as for Gohr and Koch in Zurich. Right now I am so tired I can't think."

"What's wrong, Pat? Don't you believe in me anymore?" I knew that when pressure is at its greatest, an athlete's confidence is extremely fragile. Here lies one of the greatest responsibilities of a coach, and in a coach-athlete relationship as close as Evelyn's and mine, every blink of an eye meant something. No lies could be told. In the past Evelyn had sought my reassurance, and she needed it again now.

"For cryin' out loud, I'll always believe in you, Evelyn. You won the one hundred against all odds.

It is only that I need a break from all of this too. We'll start back to work next week. The gold medal is yours."

Another coach I knew saw the predicament Evelyn was in and suggested a way to heal her leg quickly. "I know how you feel about drugs, but with so little time for Evelyn to heal, you must consider giving her small doses of steroids." As my face contorted in anger, he continued, "Don't freak out until you hear why. Before steroids were banned, some coaches and doctors used them to help rehabilitate certain injuries in record time. They were used on soldiers to heal their wounds. You have a medical reason for giving them to her now."

I'd listened long enough, "I don't believe what I am hearing. How many times will I have to say NO to drugs? Evelyn has come this far without using steroids. No way are they an option now!" The crescendo of my voice surprised us both.

"Don't you think she should make that decision?" he persisted.

"Now you sound just like Harold and Mary Anne: Let Evelyn make the decision for herself!" I mocked.

When I told this to Harold, who by now knew that Evelyn's success was a result of great coaching and superior talent and not pharmacology, he replied, "You really don't have the right to think for Evelyn. It is her gold medal on the line. You must tell her what her options are."

I slammed the door and went to bed. I was drained but too upset to sleep. Should I tell Evelyn about the drugs? Must I let her make that choice too? Why not? She was making her own decisions about everything else. (By now she excluded me from everything but her next practice.)

I phoned her. "Evelyn, please come over to my house tomorrow. I have to talk to you."

I was resting on the front porch when Ray drove Evelyn up in her new BMW. Wearing PUMAs in her races was making Evelyn a wealthy woman. A few weeks earlier, when PUMA had gotten the car for her, she'd said to me, "Do you want ten percent of my car, too?"

The proud owners of a new BMW parked across my street. They wouldn't have to push that car.

"No Evelyn, just let me test drive it to see if it is as fast as its owner." The more money she made, the more she seemed to resent paying me ten percent.

But now I wasn't thinking about money, I was thinking about drugs and how I would tell her what that coach had said.

"Hi, Evelyn. Let's go for a walk to the park." (Neither one of us could sit still when we discussed serious matters.) Ray said he'd be back after he got a haircut.

We talked about silly stuff first before I summoned the courage to say, "Evelyn, you know the sooner your leg heals, the sooner you can start training for the Olympics. Time is against us."

"I've been wondering about that myself."

"Well, there's been a suggestion. I won't tell you my opinion." Just then I said to myself, *If she chooses to take the drugs, I'll have no part of it. Ray can coach her. My goal for all these years is for her to be the best in the world, WITHOUT DRUGS.* Thinking this, I groaned out loud.

Evelyn looked at me in surprise. "Pat, what's wrong?"

"Everything. I feel an obligation to tell you that there's a doctor who can help your injured leg heal faster than . . ."

"What are you talking about?" she erupted, sensing what was coming.

"If you take steroids, your leg will heal faster. . . ." It was out.

Evelyn stopped dead in her tracks. "After all these years of saying I don't need drugs, now you are telling me to take steroids?" Tears filled her eyes. "You really don't believe in me anymore," she said, and ran away. I walked home, my heart under my feet. When Ray came back to get her, I told him what had happened. He understood that I didn't want her to take the drugs, but that I had to let her make that decision. A few hours later he found her and brought her back to my house.

I greeted her with a big hug saying, "Evelyn, never forget for one minute that I believe in you."

"Well, I'm not taking steroids or anything else," she said with the determined look that had become her trademark at the starting line. "If I can't do it on my own—without drugs—then I don't want to do anything."

I was so relieved, I grabbed her again with such newfound strength that I almost crushed her. Ray said, "Let's go into the house. We've given your neighbors enough of a show for today."

When Evelyn saw Harold, she said, "Did you put Pat up to this?"

Harold hugged her too. "You're in a tough spot, but you don't need drugs. You're naturally the greatest sprinter ever."

Ray went out to shoot baskets with Rook (Ray's name for my son Bradley) while Evelyn and I discussed our drug-free strategy for Olympic gold and a victory over the East Germans in Zurich.

By the time the Olympic flame was burning in the Los Angeles Coliseum, PUMA had rented a USC sorority house for us to stay in so we could be close to all the events. There was a big-screen TV in the living room and Ray, Evelyn, and I, along with other PUMA guests, would watch the Olympics in comfort.

The coming of the Games to Los Angeles had filled the news every day for the past year. We watched the American swimmers and gymnasts chalk up big victories. American athletes seemed to be painting our city with gold. Los Angeles had never looked more beautiful. Even the notorious traffic and smog were gone, leaving the pastel-colored Olympic flags that decorated the city to flap brightly in the summer breeze.

Our streets were filled with people visiting from over two hundred countries. From Olympic pin traders to fans at the sporting events themselves, everyone was consumed with the Games. Evelyn's parents were in town. Mary Anne flew down with her two nieces. Evelyn did a television interview where she told the world that to her "Sprinting is better than sex!"

Four tickets to every day of track-and-field cost me $2,000, but it was worth it to be able to share this spectacular occasion with Vicki, Elliot, and other friends, as well as with my family. We saw Carl Lewis win the first of his four gold medals

in the men's 100 meter in between Evelyn's preliminary rounds. On the morning of the women's 100-
meter final, Evelyn and I cheered for Joan Benoit
as she entered the stadium, winning the first women's Olympic marathon in history. Patting Evelyn
on her shoulder, I said, "The American women
have won the longest race. This afternoon another
American will win the shortest race." Then, as a
dehydrated Swiss woman stumbled into the stadium
contorted by her cramping muscles, yet determined
to finish the last 400 meters of the marathon, both
Evelyn and I stood up and cheered her on. We
yelled and identified with every agonizing step she
took to the finish line.

TV cameras were replaying Joan's entrance into
the stadium, and I said, "Look, Joanie's bra strap
is showing. I hate that. Too bad you can't wear
your racing suit."

"It's too bad the USA uniforms are so ugly."
Evelyn spoke the words I was thinking.

That afternoon, while Evelyn was warming up
before the final, I noticed *her* bra strap was showing.
I made her take it off and wadded it in my pocket.
So Evelyn's bra was history before it could make
history.

Bradley and Mary Anne were already in our seats
when I joined them. Ray was on the other side of
the stadium with Evelyn's parents, the PUMA executives, and the TV cameras. "Well, just seventeen

minutes before Evelyn is an Olympic champion," I said confidently. Harold arrived just minutes before the gun.

"How's Evelyn's leg holding up?"

"It was fine for the preliminary heats yesterday, and she felt no pain earlier today in the semifinal."

Bradley said, "She's ready," when he saw her determined face on the big TV screen by the electronic scoreboard.

Frequently looking at my watch, I said, "Yup, just forty-five seconds before she's an Olympic champ."

Harold now sat silently, remembering his 1956 Olympic victory. His hammer-throw event had lasted more than an hour, with six chances to make the winning toss. Evelyn would be at the finish line in fewer than eleven seconds from her start, with only one chance.

As the finalists stood behind their blocks, Mary Anne grabbed my hand, saying, "This is it," which made Kenny Loggins' song run through my mind.

They were off, and in less time than it will take to read this paragraph Evelyn had set a new Olympic record of 10.97. Everyone stood for her victory lap. I sat crying in relief. I did stand to watch her in the medal ceremony. At last my big-hearted little sprinter had her gold. I didn't try to find her right away because I knew she was being escorted by officials to Doping Control, there to be tested for drugs. Unlike some Olympic athletes she had noth-

Olympic victory and record in perfect form and no bra straps.

ing to worry about except the long hour it would probably take her to give a urine sample. With all the excitement, that was hard for her.

Bradley and Harold were engrossed in other Olympic events that were still being contested, but I didn't see them.

"What now?" I said to Mary Anne. She was ready with an answer. "This is the moment I've seen coming. Since 1976 I've watched your growing ties with Evelyn. You've been more than a coach; you've been her best friend. What you have to understand now is that with all the excitement—with Evelyn's relatives, her agent, her attorney, and her sponsors all demanding her attention, not to mention her new manager for her meets in Europe — she'll lose sight of you. But not on purpose. She doesn't really need a coach to train her anymore. It's all to be expected, but you can't help but feel left out and let down." Mary Anne was right.

"I don't know what to do next," I said. Harold put his arm around me and with a kiss said, "Go find Evelyn. She'll want to show her coach her medal."

Then, as the crowd filed out of the stadium, I said to Harold, Mary Anne, and Bradley, "Meet me back at PUMA House. I'll go rescue Evelyn from the press. She still has to think about the relay races to come."

I found Evelyn wandering alone with a small box in her hand. "There you are, champ. You were beautiful! Even crying on the victory stand you were just — beautiful. Let me see your medal." She took her gold medal out of the box and shyly grinned.

The crowd of reporters, officials, and spectators seemed to disappear as we clung to each other, somehow knowing it was our last shared moment of love, respect, and pure joy. Other people now had plans for Evelyn.

I watched the closing ceremonies, realizing that our Olympic dreams were now just memories. Athletes from all over the world spilled into the stadium. Some held hands forming long chains; others em-

Back at the Puma House Evelyn is all smiles as Mary Anne's niece snaps a photo.   G. Quartaroli

braced in tearful good-byes; all were swaying with the intoxicating music in a sea of bright colors. Fireworks exploded overhead. The scoreboards flashed "Farewell." Then the music and lights faded, and all eyes watched as the Olympic torch dimmed, flickered, and died.

Epilogue

Evelyn called from Zurich with news of her world-record victory over Gohr: 10.76! She phoned again when she returned from Europe to tell me she was feeling nauseated. I suggested, "Go to the doctor. You're pregnant." She rang up on May 30, 1985, with news of her beautiful five-pound baby girl. "I'll call her Raina, after Ray of course."

I've seen Raina only a few times, but I was playing with her out at the track the day she took her first baby steps.

OPPOSITE:
A hug from Diane Williams who placed third in Evelyn's world record defeat of Gohr in Zurich.

Teammates again in Seoul (1988), Karin and Evelyn pose before the opening ceremony where Evelyn was elected to carry the American flag. She won silver (100m) and gold (relay) medals, once again running down Gohr.

Fast, Faster, Fastest

Evelyn's times in the 100 meters

1975   11.60 seconds

1976   11.21 seconds

1977   11.25 seconds

1978   11.16 seconds

1979   10.97 seconds

1980   U.S. Boycotts Olympics

1981   10.90 seconds

1982   10.93 seconds

1983   10.79 seconds*

1984   10.76 seconds*

*World Record

Index

Numbers in *italics* refer to illustrations.

There are no entries for Evelyn Ashford or Pat Connolly, as they appear on almost every page.